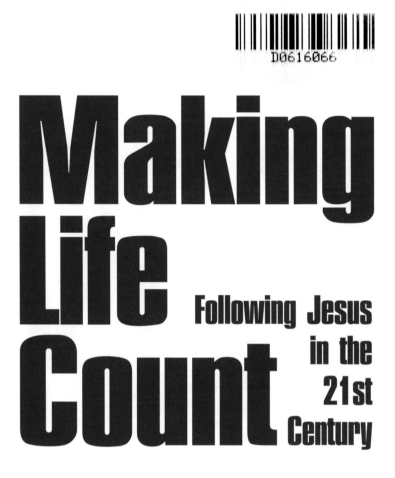

Making Life Count

Following Jesus in the 21st Century

ROBERT E. LOGAN AND TARA MILLER

ChurchSmart
RESOURCES

St. Charles, IL 60174
1-800-253-4276

Published by ChurchSmart Resources

We are an evangelical Christian publisher committed to producing excellent products at affordable prices to help church leaders accomplish effective ministry in the areas of church planting, church growth, church renewal and leadership development.

For a free catalog of our resources call 1-800-253-4276.

Visit us at: *www.churchsmart.com*

Cover design by: Julie Becker

© Copyright 2009

ISBN#: 978-1-889638-84-3

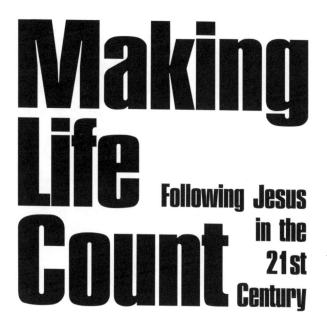

Making Life Count

Following Jesus in the 21st Century

"I went to the woods because I wished to live deliberately,
to front only the essential facts of life,
and see if I could not learn what it had to teach,
and not, when I came to die,
discover that I had not lived."
— Henry David Thoreau, from *Walden*

"All men die. Not all men really live."
— from the film *Braveheart*

All Scripture passages are TNIV
(Today's New International Version)
unless otherwise noted.

Contents

Chapter 1: recognizing the image of God 29
We are valuable, created by God in his image. We were designed as relational beings, and we were designed for a purpose, to be used by God.

Chapter 2: engaging with God.. 41
We need to cultivate intimacy with God. That can look many different ways, but needs to be intentional on our part.

Chapter 3: staying centered.. 55
To become mature personally, we must develop our character. This development of personal centeredness requires both reflection and action.

Chapter 4: journeying with others 67
We cannot live the life of a disciple in isolation—we need others along with us. That is how God designed us and why he designed the church.

Chapter 5: focusing priorities 81
We need to assess our responsibilities and listen to what God wants from us. Then we can decide what our priorities are and where we need to focus our energy.

Chapter 6: taking charge of life... 93
We need to take responsibility for our own lives. How we spend our time and energy is up to us, including what we commit to doing and how we honor our word.

Chapter 7: playing well with others 109
We need to maintain good, clear relationships with others. This means communicating well, recognizing that all people are different, and resolving conflicts directly as they arise.

Chapter 8: mastering money 123
Our money is not our own—it belongs to God. We are stewards. Therefore, we need to be both responsible and generous with our money.

Chapter 9: toppling idols 139
We need to identify the idols in our lives, then we can strategically and intentionally move them out of our lives. Within that vacant space, we can then invite God to dwell.

Chapter 10: loving our neighbor 151
Whatever our plan looks like, we need to live with an outward focus—with the compassion of Jesus toward others. We need to live with an eye toward how we can bless others, reach out, engage, listen, and love.

Chapter 11: embracing our gifts and calling 161
God's intentions for us will align with our gifts, passions, and life context. We need to discern God's voice, discover who he has made us to be, and find ways to live out our giftedness and calling.

Chapter 12: teaming with others 171
To live out our calling, we need others alongside us. None of us is complete on our own. We all have a different part to play. Therefore, we need to learn how to work well with others toward a common goal.

Chapter 13: making our kingdom contribution 183
If we live well, as a disciple of Christ, following his guidance, we will leave a legacy. We will make a difference in this world and in the lives of others, patterning our lives along the last words of Jesus.

Acknowledgements

Thank you to all of those people whose ideas and lives have helped shape our thinking, and especially those whose feedback helped strengthen this book: Lena Giron, Ray Wheeler, Michael Bischoff, Mark Miller, Carrie Hoffman, Dennis Bachman, and Jon Van Bruggen. We have also benefitted tremendously from the support provided by the CoachNet team throughout the writing process. And thanks to our publisher, ChurchSmart Resources, for their ongoing commitment to making material available that strengthens both the church and the kingdom.

FROM BOB:

As always, I appreciate the partnership and encouragement of Janet, my wife of 32 years. I'm also greatly indebted to those I walk alongside in ministry at ViaCordis and at CoachNet. And thank you to Tara, my coauthor on this book—I increasingly appreciate our partnership together. It's a privilege to team together with such wonderful people for a greater purpose.

FROM TARA:

Thanks to my husband, Mark. I can't express how much I appreciate walking through life with you. And thanks to my beautiful children, Chloe, Raina, and Amanuel. May each of you grow to be more and more the amazing people God has designed you to be. Finally, thanks to my coauthor, Bob. My experience of working with you for several years now has been but a small part of your legacy so far.

Introductions

Meet Maria, Isaac, Harry, and Sonya[1]. We'll be getting to know them better throughout the rest of this book.

Maria is in her mid-thirties, single, with three kids. Her oldest son is turning thirteen this year, and she's worried he's getting in with the wrong crowd at school. Her daughter is ten and her youngest son is nine. Maria works full time at her job in retail. She is good at connecting with people in that role and help-ing them find what they need. She also has a heart for ministry and enjoys teaching the fifth-grade Sunday school class at church. Some-day Maria would love to work in children's ministry fulltime. But she can't see how that would ever happen realistically. With three kids and a full time job, it's all she can do to keep her head above water as it is. Maria struggles with being overwhelmed with too much to do. Orga-nization has never come naturally to her, and she often does things at the last minute, whether it's her Sunday school lessons or paying the bills. If I could just get orga-nized, she thinks. But most of the time it seems like she could spend her whole life sorting and still not get to the bottom of it all. So she

> *Maria struggles with being overwhelmed with too much to do.*

just keeps going. Maria also struggles with finding the time to eat right, exercise, and take time for herself. But she's an amazing networker and bargain hunter and does an excellent job of providing for her family on limited resources. She's creative, always coming up with more ideas

---

[1] Maria, Isaac, Harry, and Sonya are fictional. Any resemblance to real persons, living or dead, is purely coincidental. However, you would not be the first person to suspect we have been spying on you and then writing about it.

than she can try out. And her connections with people, both at home and at work, help others feel heard and cared for.

Isaac is a salesman in his late twenties. He makes good money but often feels driven, constantly jumping from one thing to the next. He is always working on a deadline, under adrenaline, and at the last minute. Isaac travels for work and sets his own schedule, which tends to be random and subject to sudden changes.  His relationships suffer as a result of his busy work schedule, leading to tension and arguments with his wife. She sometimes says she's raising their three-year-old twin sons by herself and is getting frustrated with his absence. Isaac's wife is not a follower of Christ, and resents any time he spends at church, saying it's obviously not helping him anyway. Isaac has been in and out of church his whole life, but has had trouble getting settled and really becoming part of a stable community. Sometimes he's not even sure that's possible. His friends often razz him for never having time to go out and shoot pool or hang out. Isaac often feels misunderstood, like his family and friends don't understand or appreciate how hard he's working or how lonely he feels.

Isaac often feels misunderstood.

Harry is a recovering addict in his mid-forties. He's unemployed and struggles to keep his temper under control, but now that he has discovered faith in Jesus and has been clean for six months, Harry really wants to make a fresh start with his life. He showed up at a church a few weeks ago, and felt awkward  going in, like everyone would know right away that he didn't really belong there. Harry doesn't know anyone at the church yet. He would like to get connected with some other followers of Jesus, but isn't sure if the church is a safe place for that or not. "After all," he thinks, "I've done some pretty awful things in my life. And now my grown kids won't talk to me and my ex-wife hates me. Wouldn't they laugh if they saw me here at a church! I don't exactly blend in." But Harry knows that many of the people in his

Harry really wants to make a fresh start with his life.

twelve-step group are involved in churches, and they certainly don't have it all together. So he's looking. And he's wondering what, if anything, he has to offer. At forty-five years old, with his history and so much wasted time already, what could God really use him for?

Sonya is a high school social studies teacher, a single woman in her late thirties with a good heart, a generous nature, and a desire to help others. Because of these qualities, Sonya finds that people often ask her to do things—serve on this board at school, help out at this function at church, volunteer for this  event—and her default reflex is to say yes to anything that sounds like a worthy cause. The few times she has said no, she has been plagued by guilt, and so she usually ends up over-committing, taking on too much, and being unable to finish what she has started. As a result, Sonya is often overloaded with too many commitments and struggles with getting all the pieces to connect in her life. She sometimes feels like her own good intentions get in the way of her living her life. And when Sonya comes to the end of her energy, she withdraws, isolates, and worries.

Sonya is often overloaded with too many commitments.

She would like to get married someday. But what if that never happens? And trying to pay off big student loans on a teacher's salary is a major stressor. And then there's her brother, who struggles with mental illness and seems constantly in need of her help. It just seems there's never enough margin in life.

■ ■ ■

Have you ever felt like there's just not enough margin in life? Like it's hard to sort through all the demands and pressures? And there just aren't enough hours in the day to get everything done you need to do? Like you never have enough time left over to do what you really want to do in life? And like following Jesus is just one more thing to add to your already long list?

We've all been there. We all have dreams and desires, things we'd like to do. We want to see that our lives are going somewhere, counting for something. We'd like to feel close to God and others, like we're making a difference in this world, contributing our gifts and talents. We want to know that God is using us to build his kingdom. We may even want to be a leader someday. But we also have challenges and distractions, problems and obstacles. And we're often not sure how to get around them.

Most of the time it's the simple stuff that derails our discipleship.

It seems like the same old things keep tripping us up and preventing us from getting where we want to go. And most of the time it's the simple stuff that derails our discipleship: Low on time, low on money, losing track of what we were supposed to be doing. Our lives just don't seem in order. We're like a wagon in the mud: we want to move forward, but we just keep getting stuck. We start back up again, but just when it feels like we get going, we find we don't have enough traction and slip back again. Sometimes we're just spinning our wheels; other times if feels like the wheels are going to come right off.

It's like that in life. We get stuck. We lose traction. We get off course, distracted, busy, caught in the rat race. We have trouble making and then keeping our appointments. We get buried in commitments and then aren't sure what to do first. We get immobilized, unable to move forward. Our life with God suffers from lack of time. We struggle to communicate well with others. We feel overloaded and overwhelmed.

There must be another way.

There must be another way. A way to live life more fruitfully, more purposefully, more peacefully.

Imagine a man in a boat that is slowly filling up with water. He has a bucket and is working very hard to rid the boat of water. He's working up a sweat as he keeps bailing out the boat. If he keeps at it, very fast and very hard, he can just about break even with the pace of the water filling up the boat. So he can keep doing that indefinitely. Or he can go underneath and see if there's a hole he might be able to patch.

That's how our lives feel sometimes—like we're frazzled and expending so much of our energy just to break even. And we are faced with a choice: Do we keep bailing out the water or do we try to patch the hole? Do we keep struggling against a difficult reality or do we see if there's something we can do to solve the longer-term problem?

Do you want to:
- ✤ have time to do what you really want to do?
- ✤ feel like you're moving in a clear direction?
- ✤ stop feeling caught in rat race?
- ✤ know that your life is counting for something?

If that sounds more like the life you want, consider plugging the hole in the boat.

What's needed is practical discipleship. Whole life discipleship. A way of living and following Jesus in the 21st century.

What's needed is practical discipleship. Whole life discipleship. A way of living and following Jesus in the 21st century.

The goal of this book is to combine basic discipleship with basic life skills to help people achieve the kind of life they want. Will that take some effort? Yes, certainly. But the longer-term reward is huge: freedom as you learn to follow Jesus more.

WHOLE LIFE DISCIPLESHIP

Discipleship is not just praying and reading the Bible and going to church. It is living as a follower of Jesus in the real world—taking all those real pressures and real obstacles into account. When we look at the Bible, we find that God has a lot to say about living our day-to-day lives. The practical getting-things-done areas of life are not the opposite of the spiritual side of life. They are a part of it. It's not an either/or. There's no thick line between spiritual and practical. All of life is spiritual, and we are to live it—all of it—as spiritual beings.

What we focus on here in this book are practical tools for living out kingdom values. Many of us were not taught these skills growing up. But we can learn them, and we can begin to live them out. Living out kingdom values is an ongoing process for all of us. Even when we're generally doing well, we all slip backwards sometimes. We can easily turn around to find that our margins have slipped again, that we need to sift through our lives again and figure out how to move forward effectively. Being freed up to live as a disciple of Jesus is a dynamic, ongoing process.

practical tools for living out kingdom values

There are certain life skills rooted in scripture that, if we don't practice them, can prevent us from being fruitful for God's kingdom. This is a book about those areas of our lives where many of us seem to get shipwrecked most often, such as managing our time, managing our money, working with others, or staying centered. If we can tackle areas like these well, we'll be freed to be fruitful personally and be in a position to live out the bigger calling God has given us.

Although this book does focus on many of the external practices we can engage in to help us live more fruitfully, but let's be clear on where real transformation comes from: our engagement with God and others. The only way any of the ideas in this book will make a significant difference in our lives is through the Spirit of God. Sure, there are some helpful practices or wise strategies—and we all feel the need to get our lives together sometimes—but really we are on a journey with God and others. It's a relational and spiritual process of discovery.

The point of this book is not to add one more thing to our already busy lives.

Our lives with God are not all about behavior or a list of dos and don'ts. That's a horrible way to live. Nor are our lives with God a purely spiritual interior experience that has no impact on the way we live our day-to-day lives in the real world. Changed behavior is not sustainable without internal change. And internal change isn't sustainable without changed behavior. The two work in tandem: behavioral changes are rooted in our internal journey with God. And when we manage our lives well, we feel more settled and more at peace.

As writers, we recognize that this kind of life with God—both the internal and the external aspects—is both a process and a challenge. Doing and being both flow out of the deeper place of our connection with the Spirit. The types of things we write about here are issues we've dealt with ourselves—and continue to deal with. Even in the writing of this book, we've been challenged by each other's ideas. We'll share some of those stories with you along the way. Growth is definitely a process, and one that we need to return to again and again.

DEFRAGGING YOUR LIFE

The point of this book is not to add one more thing to our already **busy lives.** It's more about creating time and space *within* our lives so we'll have the ability to engage more fully with God and with others as we live out his calling.

If Isaac is already busy and tired and behind on his work, what will be helpful? Will it be helpful to get up even earlier to read the Bible and pray? Possibly. But he may just become more tired and worn out. Will it be helpful for him to work and work and work to try to get caught up? Possibly. But working without a break may make him even less productive, and less engaged with God and others. What would actually energize Isaac? Knowing Isaac, exercise, fresh air, and spiritual input. So if Isaac goes for a walk outside on his lunch break every day and listens to scripture being read aloud on his iPod, he comes back more refreshed and able to take care of his other responsibilities.

Take your computer. Technicians recommend running a "defrag" periodically to clean up a computer. The process compresses old files and reorganizes them so the computer can function faster and more efficiently. Although it could seem like taking the time to defrag is just one more thing to do, it's really something that speeds up the overall process and makes the computer run better.

A few years back I (Bob) was preparing a sermon to give at my church. I'd been thinking about my topic and praying about it for quite a while and now it was time to sit down to record and organize my thoughts. But the computer seemed to be running really slowly, dragging and taking a long time for each letter to appear. I was horrified, because this was Friday and I was supposed to preach Saturday night. I ended up having to reformat my whole computer, then reload all the software back on. It took hours. I remember thinking, "Oh Lord, why on earth would you let this happen at this particular time?"

The Lord doesn't always answer my questions—at least not directly. But this time he did. You see, I was preparing to speak on priorities. And it came to me: the computer malfunction was an illustration of how our lives are. God had let me live through how we go through the process of unloading, setting our priorities, then reloading what comes back in.

That's how life is sometimes. We're carrying around all this extra stuff that's slowing us down, and we need to take time to unload it all and then reload only what's really necessary and important. Only then are we freed up enough to move forward.

One good way to do that is to take a prayer retreat, dump out whatever is on our minds into a notebook, then slow down and listen to God. Sorting through what's important and what's not can be such a valuable process. And it's one of those things we don't do just once, but something we need to do again every once in a while. Our lives get cluttered if we don't take time to slow down, listen to God, and sort everything out.

Employing the skills and principles in this book is like defragging our lives—something we should all do periodically. And like a defragged computer has freed up enough space to accomplish what we want it to do, a defragged life is one that has freed up the space for us to serve God and others. That is the goal of this book—*not* adding one more thing to your already long to-do list.

COUNTING THE COST

So is it worth it for you to keep reading? Let's walk through a process we'll be expanding on more throughout the book: counting the cost. Economists call this a "cost-benefit analysis." For every activity you do, there are possible benefits and possible costs. For example, let's say you are deciding whether to get a dog. The benefits of getting a dog might include having a friendly pet who greets you at the door, having a companion to go walking or running with, and having a built-in home security system. However, you will also want to count the costs of getting a dog. Even if you get a dog at the pound for free, you'll still have to pay for shots, dog food, and the occasional vet bill. You'll also need to invest the time to feed it every day and take it for walks. When you've counted the cost, weighed the benefits and rewards, it's time to ask the question, "Is having a dog worth it to me?"

It's the same with this book. First you'll need to assess the potential benefits—probably by reading this introduction and scanning the table of contents and the "how to read this book" section. Then if you decide to go forward, reading it will require some time on your part. Ideally, you'll invest some more time talking over the material with people, either one-on-one or in a group.

Putting the principles into practice in your life will also likely require some effort and willingness to change. But if you decide the cost is worth it, you will then reap the benefits: learning how to set your priorities, make decisions, get organized, manage your money more effectively, engage in relationships more productively, move toward your goals, and freeing up your time to spend on what you really believe is important in your life. All of these things together will free you to be more fully the disciple that Jesus has called you to be.

> *free you to be more fully the disciple that*
> *Jesus has called you to be*

So take time now to weigh the costs and the benefits. Consider where and how you sense God calling you to grow. Maybe he has other areas for you to focus on right now and a different approach or activity might be more effective. But maybe you recognize some of the issues we've been talking about so far and you're sensing that this is exactly where God would like you to focus next.

Also consider where you are in life right now. Is this a time of crisis? Are you unusually busy? Then maybe this is not the right time to take on another commitment. However, if you find yourself chronically in crisis or always busy, investing the time to go through this book now could be your ticket to a more sane, more peaceful life down the road.

So count the cost and, if you decide to move forward, commit to doing so fully and with a hopeful, expectant heart. For those who are new to following Jesus, you can find many of the essentials here—helpful practices, essential scripture passages to become familiar with, and practical principles for getting started in a good direction. For those who have been following Jesus for a while now, focus on the areas where you're getting tripped up. Try opening your mind to new possibilities, new habits, new perspectives. Rather than glossing over a familiar scripture passage, ask the Holy Spirit to show you something new and fresh that can make a difference as you freely choose to follow Jesus.

For any of us who want to live a healthy, balanced, Christ-centered life that prepares us for whatever God may have for us, God sends us a clear message in the scriptures: there is hope. Although it may seem impossible some days, we can learn to manage our time, prioritize our lives, resolve conflicts, and work well with others. We can get traction. We can get where we want to go. We can make our lives count. There is hope.

MOVING FORWARD INTO HOPE

Think of Maria, Isaac, Sonya, and Harry. If they are able to grab hold of the concepts in this book and put them into practice, they will each be well positioned to move forward in life and ministry. Their lives will be fruitfully used by God to an even greater extent than they are now.

Living out the kingdom is never easy. It doesn't bring promises of a loving spouse, a harmonious family life, financial stability, and so on. But it does open up the possibility of living a new kind of life. A life that is honoring to God and loving toward others from here on out, no matter what the past has been like. We serve a God of grace, a God of fresh starts, a God who redeems our lives, one by one.

By God's grace, we can create a healthy, balanced, Christ-centered life that will prepare us for however God chooses to use us in the future. We are his children, beloved and created with care and purpose: "For we are God's handiwork, created in Christ Jesus to do good works, which God prepared in advance for us to do" (Ephesians 2:10).

REFLECTION QUESTIONS:

1. What is your goal in reading this book? What do you hope to accomplish?
2. What are the potential benefits?
3. How open are you to letting God change your life?
4. What support will you have from others?
5. What are you willing to invest in this journey in terms of time and energy?

How to read this book:

Making Life Count was designed to be read interactively, alongside people who will journey with you. Like the life of faith in general, it is best lived out within community. You can go through this book with a discipler or mentor, with a friend, with a cluster group of 3-4 people, or with a small group.

You may not have your life all together. That's okay—all of us struggle in different areas. So take the risk of letting others into your world. You may be surprised to find that their lives are a little untidy as well. And who knows, you may have something to offer them too.

Biblical principles and content

▼ ▼

personal reflection ◄=► **meaningful conversations with others**

▲ ▲

living out practical, biblical life skills

If you are on a desert island and have absolutely no one who will read this book with you, take time at the end of each chapter to pray, to reflect on the group discussion questions, and to complete the exercises. Like a person in an empty movie theater talking back to the characters on the screen, interact with the material as much as possible.

HOW LONG WILL IT TAKE?

Thirteen weeks. If your group meets once a week and discusses one chapter a week, you can get through all of the chapters in thirteen weeks. We've kept the chapters short to make this goal more manageable.

The three recurring themes you'll see in these thirteen chapters are God, self, and others. The book is divided into three parts, and with each part, we'll go a little further into how we look at God, self, and others. In this way, the ideas build on one another as we dig deeper and deeper into the material.

WHAT'S IN EACH CHAPTER?

We'll begin each chapter with a story about Maria, Isaac, Harry, or Sonya. You've already met them in the introduction.

Then we'll take a look at some relevant scripture passages. We'll consider the ideas in them, and discuss some practical ways to apply the biblical principles to our lives.

Periodically we'll share some of our own stories. Hopefully you'll be encouraged to know that we've struggled in many of these areas ourselves and are still growing in them.

Most chapters will also have some proverbs sprinkled throughout. Proverbs are short wisdom sayings, dedicated to wise living and filled with practical advice for daily life. Note that you have to use your head in reading proverbs. They are designed to be read in the context of life and interpreted according to the situation.

For example, two common proverbs (not in the Bible) are "many hands make light work" and "too many cooks spoil the broth." Both are true, depending on the context. As www.bartleby.com explains, "If the job to be done requires lots of unskilled labor, such as picking up trash, then many hands *do* make light work. But if the job requires intricate skill, such as cooking or writing, or if it requires a single guiding hand, then too many cooks *do* spoil the broth."

Each chapter will also include checkpoints and exercises throughout—potential action items to apply the ideas to everyday life. These are some practical ways to move forward during the week. Potentially, group members could share their experiences living these out at the beginning of the group meeting the following week.

We've included group discussion questions at the end of each chapter. If you are reading the book alone, you can use these as reflection questions, but they are primarily intended for small group discussion.

Each chapter then ends with a suggested scripture for memorization. However, feel free to choose any of the scripture passages mentioned in the chapter that are meaningful to you.

IN EACH CHAPTER, YOU'LL FIND:

- ✤ An opening story of Maria, Isaac, Harry, or Sonya
- ✤ A meditation on the chapter topic, including:
  - ○ Relevant scripture passages
  - ○ Proverbs
  - ○ Checkpoints and exercises
- ✤ Group discussion questions
- ✤ Suggested scripture for memorization

PART 1

Building Foundations: the center that holds

Before we can fully live out the life of a disciple and a life of ministry to others, we need to have a strong foundation on which to build that kind of life. The centerpieces of that foundation are knowing who we are as people created in the image of God, learning how we best connect with God, practicing staying centered in who we are in Christ, and engaging with others along the way. Knowing ourselves, God, and others and being able to stay centered in that reality creates a strong central foundation upon which to build a life of discipleship and ministry.

Chapter 1: recognizing the image of God
We are valuable, created by God in his image. We were designed as relational beings, and we were designed for a purpose, to be used by God.

Chapter 2: engaging with God
We need to cultivate intimacy with God. That can look many different ways, but needs to be intentional on our part.

Chapter 3: staying centered
To become mature personally, we must develop our character. This development of personal centeredness requires both reflection and action.

Chapter 4: journeying with others
We cannot live the life of a disciple in isolation—we need others along with us. That is how God designed us and why he designed the church.

CHAPTER 1

Recognizing the image of God

Harry had been sitting in his car in the dark church parking lot for ten minutes. *I hate going to new things, he thought to himself. I wonder what the people will be like. If they're these judgmental church types, I'm out of here. They probably won't want someone like me here anyway, so it'll be mutual. What was I thinking, anyway? Well, guess I might as well get this over with.* And Harry slammed the car door shut behind him.

Having recently gone into recovery from a drug addiction, Harry found himself suspicious of church and church people at the same time that he was feeling a strong need for God in his life. He walked into the church looking around warily, as if he wasn't supposed to be there and could be asked to leave at any time. When he entered the room where the small group was about to start, he sat down gruffly on a metal folding chair, crossed his arms, and began studying the floor. A couple of the people in the room glanced at him, unsure whether to greet him or not. One person said hi, and Harry nodded in acknowledgment.

■ ■ ■

Most of us have felt like Harry at one time or another. Like we don't belong, like if people really knew us they would want us to leave. Sometimes shame and fear can block us from the kinds of relationships with God and others that we so desperately need.

> **So much of who we are today can be traced back to the first three chapters of the book of Genesis. We are created by God, in his own image. Yet we are fallen and imperfect. Both of those conditions—created in the image of God, yet fallen—are present in us today. And they impact how we relate to God, others, and ourselves.**

Learning more about how God made us and how he views us can help us paint a more accurate, more helpful portrait of ourselves. In this chapter, we'll take a look at how God created us, what went wrong, and the purpose he has for us.

CREATED IN THE IMAGE OF GOD

Genesis 1:26-28 says:

> Then God said, "Let us make human beings in our image, in our likeness, so that they may rule over the fish in the sea and the birds in the sky, over the livestock and all the wild animals, and over all the creatures that move along the ground." So God created human beings in his own image, in the image of God he created them; male and female he created them. God blessed them and said to them, "Be fruitful and increase in number; fill the earth and subdue it. Rule over the fish in the sea and the birds in the sky and over every living creature that moves on the ground."

As the final step of his creation, God created people. And unlike any of his other creations—birds, fish, plants, or animals—God created human beings in his own image. That means there is something inside every single human being that reflects God. There is dignity simply in being human, because humans are created in the image of God.

A lot of different kinds of people make up the world: men and women, children and adults, different races and culture groups. And we are all made in the image of God. According to verse 27, both men and women were created in the image of God. That image was then passed on to their children, who spread out to populate the whole globe (v. 28). All nations, races, and cultures descended from Adam and Eve.

There is dignity simply in being human.

We all live as image-bearers of God. The New Testament later underscores the equality of all in Jesus Christ: "So in Christ Jesus you are all children of God through faith, for all of you who were baptized into Christ have clothed yourselves with Christ. There is neither Jew nor Gentile, neither slave nor free, neither male nor female, for you are all one in Christ Jesus. If you belong to Christ, then you are Abraham's seed, and heirs according to the promise" (Galatians 3:26-29).

So what does it mean to be created in the image of God? In part, it means we each reflect something about him to others. We each reflect him differently, and we reflect different parts of his character. But if we look deeply into ourselves or others, we can find something of God there. There are traces of his fingerprints on each one of us. Every person created in the image of God has dignity and is worthy of respect.

RELATIONAL BEINGS

Being created in the image of God also means we are relational by our very nature. After all, God himself is relational. The three persons of the trinity—the Father, the Son, and the Holy Spirit—existed from the beginning. Together they created people to reflect themselves: "Let *us* make human beings in *our* image."

And God did not create just one person, but two. When there was just Adam, God observed, "It is not good for the man to be alone" (Genesis 2:18). So he created Eve. Then he commanded them to multiply. Throughout history, we have lived in groups: families, tribes, the nation of Israel, the church. We were designed as relational beings from the beginning. We don't do well in isolation—we need each other.

THE FALL

But then there was the fall. God said not to eat the fruit. But Adam and Eve, given free will, chose to eat it anyway. And immediately they felt shame and fear, which have been hallmarks of fallen people ever since.

The fall is what made life so difficult. Suddenly, we had to work hard because problems kept arising. Things did not go according to plan, and we ran into obstacles and even death: "Cursed is the ground because of you; through painful toil you will eat of it all the days of your life. It will produce thorns and thistles for you, and you will eat the plants of the field. By the sweat of your brow you will eat your food until you return to the ground, since from it you were taken; for dust you are and to dust you will return" (Genesis 3:17-19).

Food no longer grows naturally without effort or care. If we want to have a garden now, it's no Eden. We have to plant, water, tend, fertilize, and weed. And sometimes it still doesn't produce the fruit we want.

The fall is also why living as a follower of Christ is hard. Doing what's right no longer comes naturally. But the desire is still within us somewhere... where the image of God dwells in us. So there is hope.

> I do not understand what I do. For what I want to do I do not do, but what I hate I do. And if I do what I do not want to do, I agree that the law is good. As it is, it is no longer I myself who do it, but it is sin living in me. I know that good itself does not dwell in me, that is, in my sinful nature. For I have the desire to do what is good, but I cannot carry it out. For I do not do the good I want to do, but the evil I do not want to do—this I keep on doing. Now if I do what I do not want to do, it is no longer I who do it, but it is sin living in me that does it.
>
> So I find this law at work: Although I want to do good, evil is right there with me. For in my inner being I delight in God's law; but I see another law at work in me, waging war against the law of my mind and making me a prisoner of the law of sin at work within me. What a wretched man I am! Who will rescue me from this body of death? Thanks be to God, who delivers me through Jesus Christ our Lord! (Romans 7:15-25)

WONDERFULLY MADE

But in spite of the fall, the image of God remains. Just because we're fallen, it doesn't mean we can't do anything good. If we think about it, we've all seen people do good things—even great things.

I (Bob) have seen people, complete strangers, treating my elderly father with kindness. My father suffers from Parkinson's disease and scoliosis and is bent over. Yet I see people willing to help, even though they've never met the man. They look at him with care, consideration, and respect. It's amazing how perfect strangers will care. And their acts of kindness are a reflection of the image of God.

When someone does something creative—an artist who creates a painting or a musician who writes a song—that's part of the reflection of the image of God as well. In that way, we reflect God's creativity. Even those that aren't yet connected to God in relationship through Jesus are still created in his image and therefore reflect something of him.

> *When we see the good in ourselves or others, it's a reflection of the God who created us.*

We also reflect God through the presence of a human spirit inside each one of us. God is Spirit, and ultimately it is our spirit that connects us with God. Sometimes Alzheimer's patients, even when they can't recognize people or recall facts, are able to recognize Scripture and hymns. Even when the mind isn't functioning, the spirit is present. Just as we see God in those who are not followers of Christ performing heroic acts, such as the firefighters on 9/11, we also see God when we see that all people demonstrate the universal capability to recognize and connect with the spiritual realm.

Even though we're fallen, when we see the good in ourselves or others, it's a reflection of the God who created us. He made every one of us unique and special. Not only did God create Adam and Eve, but he created each one of us with great care, designing us while we were still inside our mother's womb. And as it was in the story of creation, here again God says that it is good. As part of his creation, we are fearfully and wonderfully made. We are valuable and loved in the sight of God and he knows every hair on our heads.

For you created my inmost being; you knit me together in my mother's womb. I praise you because I am fearfully and wonderfully made; your works are wonderful, I know that full well. (Psalm 139:13-14)

Someone once said, "God don't make no junk." No matter what we do or where we've been, every one of us was created specially by God. Therefore, we are loved and valuable.

Seeing ourselves the way God sees us frees us to reach out to him and others.

Seeing ourselves as God sees us is important. Not so we can think we're wonderful when we're not—and not so we can despair over how awful and hopeless we are. In a sense, both of those views are self-focused. But seeing ourselves the way God sees us frees us to reach out to him and others. The way we view ourselves is lived out in all of our relationships.

> For by the grace given me I say to every one of you: Do not think of yourself more highly than you ought, but rather think of yourself with sober judgment, in accordance with the faith God has distributed to each of you. (Romans 12:3)

We are not to think of ourselves too highly or too lowly, but with sober and accurate judgment. We are not to be arrogant, placing ourselves above God and others, failing to take responsibility for our faults and our growth. Likewise, we are not to think too lowly of ourselves, or we may find ourselves not offering to God and others what he created us to contribute. And we are created to contribute something.

PROVERBS:

✤ Ecclesiastes 11:5: As you do not know the path of the wind, or how the body is formed in a mother's womb, so you cannot understand the work of God, the Maker of all things.[2]

---

[2] Although most of the proverbs quoted in this book are found in the book of Proverbs, some others are found in Ecclesiastes. Both books are part of what is known as "wisdom literature" within the Bible.

CHECKPOINTS:

Look for traces of the image of God in others.

❏ Reflect on evidence of the image of God in yourself.

❏ Become more aware of ways others are different from you. List some of the ways you see the image of God there.

❏ Treat others with respect and dignity, as people created in the image of God.

❏ Treat yourself with respect and dignity, as someone created in the image of God.

EXERCISES:

➤ Read through the first three chapters of Genesis once a day for three days. What stands out to you at first? What stands out to you on the second and third readings? What elements of yourself can you see in this passage?

➤ This week, when you notice the image of God in people, point out specific qualities about them that you appreciate or admire. Watch their responses.

DESIGNED FOR A PURPOSE

We have the potential to contribute to this world, to make a difference. The seeds of potential are present in each one of us to make a difference for the kingdom of God. We were designed for a purpose, to be used by God for good. The Spirit of God working within us does his work of transformation to help us reach the full potential placed within us.

Jesus told this parable: "The kingdom of heaven is like a mustard seed, which a man took and planted in his field. Though it is the smallest of all seeds, yet when it grows, it is the largest of garden plants and becomes a tree, so that the birds come and perch in its branches" (Matthew 13:31-32).

All of the potential is in the seed—God placed it there to begin with. Each seed has the possibility within it of becoming a huge tree. The amount of potential we recognize in ourselves makes a big difference in how much we grow and how much we allow God to use us.

Even as kids, certain statements or events shape our self-image. We listen to the voices of others and take in what is said, whether it's true or not. Some statements may be extreme: "You'll never amount to anything." And we grow up believing that, and—as a result—never try to amount to anything.

As a child I (Tara) remember my dad telling me and my sister that no one should ever pick on us at school: "You stand up for yourself. No one should ever treat you badly. That's not okay." And later, when we were in our 20s, my sister said to me, "I've been hearing about so many boyfriends who are hitting their girlfriends. No guy has even tried that with me. I think we must just send off an unconscious signal that tells men that would not be okay."

Not all of us have received such positive messages as children. We may not believe we're smart, beautiful, worth loving, capable, or worthy of respect. So whatever positive messages we have not taken in as children, we'll need to work toward believing based on scripture. This "reprogramming" of our minds and hearts is more difficult than it may sound, but it is possible.

In the area of learning, self-image is especially critical. A first-grade teacher talked about the importance of the years of kindergarten through second grade. She said that by third grade, if children haven't had positive experiences around learning, they start saying things like, "I can't...." They begin believing that they are not smart or cannot learn. Yet even at that point, involvement and positive interaction can make a big difference. With support, those third graders can begin to turn around and rebuild a sense of confidence in learning. It's harder, but it's possible.

The process of growth is miraculous and mysterious (how did the seed become a tree?). Yet it is also a product of predictable causes (fertilizer, rain, sunshine—and nobody coming by with a big ax).

> ## We can choose to cooperate with God's process or we can try to shut it down.

The same is true in our own lives. God is the source of growth and life—the Holy Spirit is at work in mysterious ways. *And* we can do certain things either to nurture growth or to hinder it. We can choose to bring fertilizer or an ax. Like Adam and Eve, we have free will, and our choices will make a difference. We can choose to cooperate with God's process or we can try to shut it down.

God created us to accomplish something for his purposes. What that is will look somewhat different on different people, but God has a vision for each one of us. He has created us in his image and given us spiritual gifts to carry out his kingdom here on earth. Yes, we likely have some work to do, some areas of our lives that need attention. But in spite of our flaws, God does have a purpose for us. He wants to use us. And the starting point for being used by God is learning to respect ourselves and others as sons and daughters of God, created by him.

Checkpoints:

- ❏ Look through some of the scripture passages cited in this chapter and affirm three positive things about yourself that are true based on those passages. Spend some time meditating on these scriptures to internalize them.
- ❏ Think of an area where you feel you can't be used by God. Consider whether that's true or not—according to scripture.
- ❏ Create a plan for "reprogramming" one area of your life.
- ❏ Think of five positive traits you can recognize in others that could encourage them to live up to their full potential.

■ ■ ■

Over the next few months, Harry kept going to the group at church. It was hard and sometimes he wanted to quit, but he decided to keep attending. Slowly, as people got to know him better, he noticed that they pointed out some positive things in his life. He wasn't sure whether to believe them at first. After all, they  might just be trying to be polite or flatter him, he thought. But eventually, he couldn't deny that the people in the group seemed genuine. And they genuinely seemed to like him—even when they didn't necessarily like everything he did or said.

One man from the group invited him over to watch a basketball game. At first Harry said no. Then later he regretted it and wished he'd said yes. Maybe he wouldn't be invited again. Maybe that was his only chance. But a couple weeks later, another guy invited him to play cards with him and a couple other guys from the group. And this time, Harry accepted the invitation. And as he got to know them, he found that really, they weren't as different from him as he'd thought. They were just regular guys, and fun to be around.

Three months later, Harry was out at a coffee shop with Steve, one of the leaders of his small group. They were laughing about how Harry felt when he first came to the group. "I was so sure everybody there had their life all together," remembered Harry. "I thought people would judge me and see me as different than them. And there are some differences, but by and large, I've come to see that they all have their issues too. Maybe not drugs, like me, but there's always something we need to be growing in."

"I'm glad you felt accepted, Harry," said Steve. "I know it took a lot of courage for you to come to the group at all. And at first, you weren't exactly the easiest person to reach out to." Steve stopped and smiled. "I'm glad some of the others were able to look past your gruffness at the beginning and see that you really did want to get to know them. It just didn't look like it right away."

"Thanks, I guess," muttered Harry. "I'm not sure if that's exactly a compliment."

"Actually, one of the reasons I wanted to talk with you today is because you understand how hard it is to be new. I wanted to ask if you'd be willing to watch for new people who come to our group and reach out to them, try to make them feel at home."

"Really? Me?"

"You're actually very good at that, I've noticed. Maybe you'll see it too as you do it more."

GROUP DISCUSSION QUESTIONS:

1. How does the way you view yourself line up with the scripture passages in this chapter? Which passage stood out to you most?

2. What ideas in this chapter do you relate to? What ideas seem unfamiliar or surprising to you?

3. In what ways do you view yourself more lowly or more highly than you ought?

4. What are some of the ways your view of yourself gets in the way of how you relate to God or others?

5. Which people in your life do you find it hard to relate to? How can you use the scripture passages in this chapter to find a point of connection?

SUGGESTED SCRIPTURE TO MEMORIZE:

For you created my inmost being; you knit me together in my mother's womb. I praise you because I am fearfully and wonderfully made; your works are wonderful, I know that full well. (Psalm 139:13-14)

CHAPTER 2

Engaging with God

Sonya has been going to church most of her life. She's heard many, many sermons on the importance of taking time to be with God. In the churches she has attended, the emphasis is on prayer and Bible study. Every day for fifteen minutes, preferably in the morning, each person is supposed to read the Bible and  pray. Sonya usually hears this practice referred to as a quiet time or devotions and it is to be holy time set apart from the rest of the day for the purpose of being with God.

> **She began feeling like her quiet time was a favor to God—something he needed but she didn't.**

For a while, when she was a teenager, she was really good at it. Sonya had her quiet time every morning as she read her way through the New Testament. She was proud of being a disciplined person and of doing what was expected of her. Then in her twenties, it stopped working. Her routine began to feel dry and rote. She got bored and felt more and more like she was forcing herself to go through the motions. This growing awareness of boredom made Sonya feel guilty, which then made it even harder for her to get up early to pray and read the

Bible. She began feeling like her quiet time was a favor to God—something he needed but she didn't. It was just one more item on her list of things to do, something she could check off with a sigh of relief when she was finished. Another task accomplished.

■ ■ ■

Sometimes we confuse engagement with God with certain standard practices. That's like confusing a school building with learning. One is the means; the other is the end. One is the ultimate goal; the other is simply a way to get there—and probably not the only way to get there.

Attending classes in a school building can be an excellent way to learn. It has been effective for many people. But throughout history there have been other ways to learn as well. Many parents have taught their children at home. Some have been taught by private tutors. Socrates took his students to live with him and taught them through asking them thought-provoking questions and promoting dialogue. Frederick Douglass, a runaway slave, taught himself to read and then educated himself. Many students in remote rural areas are now being educated online. For virtually any goal, there is more than one way to get there. Some are harder, some are easier, and some work better for different people.

> The message of this chapter is a simple one: Find a way to engage with God and then do it. Find a way that works, a way that refuels you and gets you in touch with God's presence, then practice that regularly and intentionally. And if it stops working, try a new way. Sometimes we need different methods for different stages of life. And sometimes we just need variety.

The bottom line is that we were created to desire intimacy with God. Something at the core of who we were created to be desires it.

Something at the core of who we were created to be desires intimacy with God.

We're not always aware of that desire—especially if we're approaching God in a way that isn't natural to us—but something in us craves interaction with the Spirit of God. And we need the many benefits that relational connection with him provides us.

CHRISTIANITY: RELATIONSHIP OR CREED?

Before we look at the many different ways we can engage with God, let's ask a different question: *Why* should we engage with God?

Jesus' message was not about starting a new religion or establishing a new set of laws. His message was an invitation to come into relationship with himself: "Let anyone who is thirsty come to me and drink. Whoever believes in me, as Scripture has said, rivers of living water will flow from within them" (John 7:37-38). Jesus positions himself as the source of life. When we commit to following Jesus, we are committing to a relationship, not just a creed.

A personal relationship provides benefits that a creed cannot. We cry out to God. We cast our cares on him. We draw strength from him. The psalmist writes, "As the deer pants for streams of water, so my soul pants for you, my God. My soul thirsts for God, for the living God. When can I go and meet with God?" (Psalm 42:1-2).

Our souls thirst for a relationship with God that creeds, laws, and religious traditions alone cannot satisfy. We need more.

WE NEED GOD

Needing is not fun. Most of us prefer being self-sufficient. After all, if we need others, then they can let us down. Better not to need. However, the truth is we do need other and we do need God. We don't do very well on our own. Since we do need, we may as well admit it.

- ✤ We need God in order to be filled and reenergized (John 7:37-38).
- ✤ We need God in order to satisfy our desire for emotional connection (Psalm 42:1-2).
- ✤ We need God to draw strength from in difficult times (2 Corinthians 12:9-10, Philippians 4:13).
- ✤ We need God in order to grow spiritually and become mature (Ephesians 4:13).
- ✤ We need God in order to serve others (1 John 4:19).

One of our biggest blockages, both personally and in our ministry to others, is not cultivating intimacy with God. God is the root of our spiritual life and the root of our ministry. We love because he first loved us. Without those roots, reaching deep down into the Holy Spirit to bring in water and nutrients, the whole plant withers and dies.

> A voice says, "Cry out." And I said, "What shall I cry?" "All men are like grass, and all their glory is like the flowers of the field. The grass withers and the flowers fall, because the breath of the LORD blows on them. Surely the people are grass. The grass withers and the flowers fall, but the word of our God stands forever" (Isaiah 40:6-8).

We need God, not the other way around.

Sometimes we find ourselves believing that time spent with God is a favor to him, something that makes him feel better. Yet in reality, God does not *need* us to do this. Our "quiet times" or "devotional times" do not stroke his ego or fuel him. Intimacy with God is not a matter of duty or doing the right thing. Although it honors him, it's not for his benefit, but for our own. We need God, not the other way around.

PROVERBS:

✤ Proverbs 1:7: The fear of the LORD is the beginning of knowledge, but fools despise wisdom and instruction.

✤ Proverbs 21:30: There is no wisdom, no insight, no plan that can succeed against the LORD.

CHECKPOINTS:

❏ Get in touch with your need for God. List some of the ways you need him.

❏ When you notice yourself giving to others, stop to reflect on the source of that energy.

❏ List some of the false beliefs you have about meeting with God.

WHAT ENGAGING WITH GOD LOOKS LIKE

Most of us have a very definite idea of what engaging with God looks like, and it's often a very narrow picture. If we are lucky, our idea of engaging with God lines up with how he has wired us. But for many of us, that's not the case. And when our idea of how we are supposed to engage with God doesn't line up with how we actually do engage with God, the result is usually guilt.

Guilt in the presence of God has a long history. It goes all the way back to the garden of Eden. And sometimes guilt is warranted. When we have done something truly wrong, our conscience is there to guide us back on track by way of repentance.

However, guilt that is rooted in artificial "shoulds" doesn't fall into that category of healthy guilt.

Beware of the artificial "should."

For example:

- ✤ Maria feels guilty when she doesn't sense God's presence when reading Christian books that have touched others deeply. She feels like something is wrong with her when a particular book recommended so highly by her friend does not have the same impact on her.

- ✤ Harry feels guilty when he doesn't enjoy the worship at his church. He has always liked secular rock music, and the traditional hymns at his church just don't do much for him. He wonders if maybe that means he's just not spiritual enough yet.

- ✤ Isaac feels guilty that he has no sense of God in the rugged mountains that everyone else seems to adore. They talk about meeting God there, while Isaac feels like he is more likely to meet God in the city, where the people are. He sees God in the people he talks with and in the stories of their lives.

God designed us as individuals; not everyone connects with him in the same ways. We have different levels of enjoyment in reading, in music, in nature, in solitude. The truth is that engagement with God looks different for different people. Feeling like we should be a certain way when we are not does nothing but bring on guilt that damages our relationship with God.

PERSONALIZING OUR RELATIONSHIP WITH GOD

Here's the secret: Find out what works for you and do that. Personalize your relationship with God. Find ways to engage with him. Find ways to become more aware of where the Holy Spirit is already present and at work.

Find out what works for you and do that.

As easy as it would be to say, "Every follower of Jesus should do X, Y, and Z in this particular way and they will grow," that just isn't the way it works. Different people tend to engage better with God through different spiritual practices. I (Tara) sense God's presence most when I engage with the characters and stories in literature and film, while my husband borrows rituals from other Christian traditions, such as prayer beads and centering prayer.

Some connect to God's presence through study, intellect, thought, and observation of the natural world. Some connect with God through interior experience and emotion. Some connect with God through action and obedience. None of these approaches is the right way, just as none of them is the wrong way. They are simply different ways.

If we relate best through study, intellect, thought, and the observation of nature, we should definitely engage in spiritual practices that align with that way of experiencing God. And in those areas where we are not naturally strong—for we will each have some of those areas—we can rely on the larger body of Christ.

As one woman said, "I find it boring to stretch in my areas of weakness spiritually. So how I do my stretching is to accept instruction and input from my Christian brothers and sisters who are strong in my weak areas. It makes me connect with them if I want to get a complete picture of something. It keeps me humble to acknowledge my limitations and it keeps me honoring other people for their strengths. I consider it a flaw to throw focus off of my strong points to try to focus on my weak areas. That's just been unhelpful for me. Instead I focus on making my strengths as strong as they can possibly be, and rely on others to shore up my weak areas. I find spiritual balance within the larger body of Christ."

Consider the following spiritual practices:*

✦ meditation	✦ prayer	✦ fasting
✦ study	✦ simplicity	✦ solitude
✦ submission	✦ service	✦ confession
✦ worship	✦ guidance	✦ celebration

Note: Each of these practices can be lived out in an almost infinite number of ways. For example, confession can be to a friend, to a group, to clergy, to God, and/or to oneself. Likewise, simplicity for one family may mean going from two cars to one; for another family, it may mean cutting out TV. The practices as listed here are intended to be general so they can be adapted to the individual.

Some of these spiritual practices will come more naturally to you. Others will not. Be open to the work of the Holy Spirit as you explore. Regularly engage in those practices that bring you closer to God. And periodically engage with other followers of Christ to stretch your understanding and experience of God in ways that will bring you to new—if sometimes uncomfortable—places.

As we continue to grow and expand the ways we are able to experience God, we can look for ways to incorporate him into the activities and routines of our everyday life. For our experience of God is not only in the "time set aside," but in the everydayness of life. We can invite God to join us in our everyday, moment-by-moment activities, such as:

✦ listening to music	✦ reading
✦ experiencing nature	✦ exercising
✦ going for a walk	✦ talking with people
✦ working with our hands	✦ driving
✦ sharing a meal	

By inviting God into our everyday life, we acknowledge that he is ever-present. We can use our five senses to experience him more deeply—in the smell of the outdoors, the sound of laughter, the taste of a good meal.

Opening up our whole lives to God, not just certain set-aside times, can be especially important for us during times of stress or transition. When one woman had a baby, she found that her traditional morning quiet times no longer worked. Instead of feeling guilty or trying harder, she found another way to feel closer to God relationally during this season. She took a half-hour walk with the stroller every morning while meditating on God. The baby loved it and the woman discovered a new aspect of her relationship with God.

> # *God is not limited to one place,*
> # *or one time of day, or one activity.*

God is not limited to one place, or one time of day, or one activity. He is everywhere. And he has provided many ways for us to experience him more fully. Meeting with God is not a matter of adding one more thing to our already full lives. It is a matter of recognizing him where he already is.

PROVERBS:

❖ Proverbs 3:5-6: Trust in the LORD with all your heart and lean not on your own understanding; in all your ways acknowledge him, and he will make your paths straight. (NIV)

CHECKPOINTS:

❑ Think of one new way this week you can invite God into your everyday life.

❑ Create a plan for connecting with God during an upcoming transition in your life.

❑ Find a person who exercises a spiritual practice different from yours. Listen and learn from their descriptions. If possible, observe them in their practice.

❑ Listen to the Holy Spirit for any ways he might be speaking to you.

THE BEAUTY OF INTENTIONALITY

God is present not only in our "time set aside" but in our whole life. So does this mean we don't need to be intentional? Not at all. When we do nothing, we usually drift away from God rather than toward him. Although our engagement with God can look many different ways, it needs to be intentional on our part.

Let's look at the example Jesus set for us. Nowhere in the gospel accounts of his life does it say Jesus had a daily quiet time. He was not ritualistic, yet he was intentional. He prayed and he communed with the Father: "Very early in the morning, while it was still dark, Jesus got up, left the house and went off to a solitary place, where he prayed" (Mark 1:35).

Jesus set an example of communion with the Father. We don't see a ritual (e.g. fifteen minutes every morning); we see a pattern of intentionality. When Jesus was pushed and pulled every which way, he took time to spend with the Father to sort out priorities. Sometimes we feel like that too—pushed and pulled in so many different directions at once. Yet we look to Jesus as our example of one who, when faced with the pressing needs of the masses, still spent time with the Father. After he fed a crowd of five thousand people with five loaves of bread and two fish, "immediately Jesus made the disciples get into the boat and go on ahead of him to the other side, while he dismissed the crowd. After he had dismissed them, he went up on a mountainside by himself to pray. When evening came, he was there alone" (Matthew 14:22-23).

As you read this chapter, don't be discouraged. None of us get it all together at one time. Engagement with God is an ongoing cultivation. The whole process is a spiritual journey.

As we fight the tyranny of the urgent, we discover how best to relate with God, dialogue with him, and keep making progress. We are always growing and journeying, and we have the opportunity to be before God as we celebrate the good and process the painful. Connection with God allows us to keep perspective.

PROVERBS:

✤ Proverbs 14:22: Do not those who plot evil go astray? But those who plan what is good find love and faithfulness.

A WORD ON SCRIPTURE

As we think about the different ways we can be intentional about engaging with God, we should stop to acknowledge the unique place scripture holds. Scripture is God's communication to us, and the foundation for our listening for his voice. Anything he says to us will be in alignment with what he says in scripture.

And yet, not all of us are wired to be readers. Many of us have had a hard time connecting with God through reading the Bible. Some of this difficulty may lie in our approach. Not all ways of reading are the same. Just like prayer, we need to find a way that works for us. Here are some ideas for engaging with scripture. Experiment and discover what works for you.

+ Classic reading and study—a chapter at a time
+ Overview reading—skimming quickly through whole books of the Bible
+ Reflective meditation on a single verse at a time
+ Memorization
+ Listening to scripture being read aloud (an audio recording can work well for this)
+ Dialoguing about scripture passages with others
+ Use your imagination to place yourself in the scene when you are reading scripture

In whatever way God communicates best to each of us, we need to engage intentionally with scripture. This is the word of the Lord. "All Scripture is God-breathed and is useful for teaching, rebuking, correcting and training in righteousness, so that all God's people may be thoroughly equipped for every good work" (2 Timothy 3:16-17).

We cannot force connection with God.

AWARENESS OF DEPENDENCE

Engaging with God—through prayer, through scripture, through innumerable ways—gives us perspective. And with perspective, we come full circle: back to our need and desire for God. We cannot make spiritual growth happen. We cannot force connection with God. He is in charge, not us. Jesus used this example:

> This is what the kingdom of God is like. A man scatters seed on the ground. Night and day, whether he sleeps or gets up, the seed sprouts and grows, though he does not know how. All by itself the soil produces grain—first the stalk, then the head, then the full kernel in the head. As soon as the grain is ripe, he puts the sickle to it, because the harvest has come (Mark 4:26-29).

The gardener, for all her work and effort and care, is not in charge. She is dependent on the rain, the sun, the miracle of growth. Her role is to plant and tend, to be listening and watching, aware of the changing weather, attuned to the bigger picture. If an early frost is in the forecast, she'll need to cover the rose bushes. But she can't force them to grow bigger or faster.

Like the gardener, we need to cultivate intimacy with God. That cultivation can look many different ways, but needs to be intentional on our part. In the same way, although we are not in charge of our own spiritual growth, we are responsible to work in concert with what God is doing, staying in tune with what's going on outside of ourselves, seeing the bigger picture and taking our cues from that. And in doing so, we will cultivate a relationship with Jesus, who satisfies our needs. "Then Jesus declared, 'I am the bread of life. Whoever comes to me will never go hungry, and whoever believes in me will never be thirsty'" (John 6:35).

■ ■ ■

After spending a few months feeling guilty, Sonya was talking with a friend of hers who mentioned that she felt closest to God when she was running. Sonya was surprised, and initially wrote the idea off as unspiritual. But Dana's comment stuck with her. Sonya respected Dana and found she couldn't easily write  off what she'd shared. Finally, she called Dana and asked her to get coffee and tell her about this whole running thing. "This is ridiculous. I don't even like running!" thought Sonya as she drove to the coffee shop where they were meeting.

And it was true—Sonya did not like running. But as she listened to how Dana experienced God, she realized that she'd been boxing God in, keeping her view of him too small and confined. God could engage with his people in many different ways and was not limited to a quiet time of Bible reading and prayer. He was much bigger than that. Sonya found herself a bit scared by that thought. Was this heresy? Did it mean she didn't value prayer or scripture? She was hesitant, but decided to give it a try to experience God in different ways.

Over time, Sonya realized that although she didn't like running or exercise (and found little of God there) she did enjoy solitude and service. Quiet and unassuming by nature, she had been raised in a tradition that encountered God primarily through reason and understanding. Even the type of prayer she'd been taught was quite structured and intellectual. But Sonya found herself drawn to the less structured experience of solitude. She began practicing centering prayer, which was wordless. She also found she could see God well in the faces of the elderly in a nearby nursing home. As she served them, she felt closer to God.

And then something strange happened. Sonya found herself enjoying reading scripture again. What had previously felt like a chore was now fresh again, as her experience of God had broadened.

GROUP DISCUSSION QUESTIONS:

1. In what ways do you relate to God most easily? In what ways do you have difficulty connecting with God?

2. What would it look like to try to engage with God in a way that is outside of your comfort zone but may be more natural to you? What would be the risks?

3. What does it look like for you to be intentional, but not ritualistic?

4. When are you most aware of your need for God? What does this tell you?

5. When are you most likely to feel guilt? How can you move closer to God then?

SUGGESTED SCRIPTURE TO MEMORIZE

Trust in the LORD with all your heart and lean not on your own understanding; in all your ways acknowledge him, and he will make your paths straight. (Proverbs 3:5-6, NIV)

CHAPTER 3

Staying Centered

Isaac is driving home from work late again. He knows what he's going to find even before he gets in the door. Tasha will be angry, the twins will be wound up and hungry, dinner will be cold or not made at all, and the house will be a disaster. Isaac can feel himself getting angry already. Why can she not appreciate how hard  he's working to support this family? Most wives would be grateful for someone like him! She just doesn't understand how stressful his job is. Instead she expects him to get right to work when he comes home too, as if he's been vacationing all day.

As Isaac pulls into the driveway, he can feel his defenses sliding into place. Yes, he had to stay late to finish that sales call. He's been working hard all day. What has Tasha been doing? She'd better not start in right away. Squaring his shoulders, Isaac walks into the house.

■ ■ ■

Getting centered is hard.
Staying centered is even harder.

WHAT DOES IT EVEN MEAN TO BE CENTERED?

Centeredness is the outflow of our connectedness with Jesus. The more we engage with God and take time to reflect on our lives, the more we are able to stay centered when difficult times come. If we have the foundation of deep connection with God and perspective, and allow him to change us and how we see things, then we're able to stay centered even in the face of difficulty.

Our relationship with God takes place inside of us, yet when we are centered, others around us see the difference. Centered people are able to keep their temper in check, not be swayed by every changing opinion, carry on in spite of adversity, and remain true to what they believe. Centered people know who they are and what they are about.

Almost anyone can be centered when times are good. But when the wind blows and the rain comes, that's when our character is tested; that's when we see how solid our foundation is.

> Therefore everyone who hears these words of mine and puts them into practice is like a wise man who built his house on the rock. The rain came down, the streams rose, and the winds blew and beat against that house; yet it did not fall, because it had its foundation on the rock. But everyone who hears these words of mine and does not put them into practice is like a foolish man who built his house on sand. The rain came down, the streams rose, and the winds blew and beat against that house, and it fell with a great crash. (Matthew 7:24-27)

That's what this chapter is about: building our life on a strong foundation. Staying centered when difficult times come requires personal reflection, management of our emotions, and life balance. These practices then result in our living a changed life—a life that reflects Jesus to the world. We will become mature in Christ:

> So Christ himself gave the apostles, the prophets, the evangelists, the pastors and teachers, to equip his people for works of service, so that the body of Christ may be built up until we all reach unity in the faith and in the knowledge of the Son of God and become mature, attaining to the whole measure

of the fullness of Christ. Then we will no longer be infants, tossed back and forth by the waves, and blown here and there by every wind of teaching and by the cunning and craftiness of people in their deceitful scheming, (Ephesians 4:11-14)

The connectedness with God that we discussed in the first chapter is focused more on the relational side—us and God. The centeredness we talk about here has its roots in our relationship with God, but is expressed as we interface with others.

Centeredness is expressed as we interface with others.

As we remain centered in Christ, we bear the fruit of the Spirit: love, joy, peace, patience, kindness, goodness, faithfulness, gentleness, and self-control (Galatians 5:22). We get back fruit according to the deposits we make. That foundation allows us to abide in Christ even in the responses of the moment.

PERSONAL REFLECTION

Centeredness requires times of reflection. Taking time to reflect sounds so simple. Stop and think: What's going well? What's not? What might I want to do differently? It sounds simple and it is. The hard part is actually doing it—being intentional about slowing down enough to reflect.

Reflection is not only simple; it's biblical. Many different voices in the Bible call us to reflection for various reasons.

We reflect to gain wisdom: "Reflect on what I am saying, for the Lord will give you insight into all this" (2 Timothy 2:7).

We reflect to line up our actions with our beliefs: "Do not merely listen to the word, and so deceive yourselves. Do what it says. Those who listen to the word but do not do what it says are like people who look at their faces in a mirror and, after looking at themselves, go away and immediately forget what they look like" (James 1:22-24).

We reflect to bring ourselves to repentance: "Because they consider all the offenses they have committed and turn away from them, they will surely live; they will not die." (Ezekiel 18:28).

We reflect to gain perspective by seeing our lives in context of the bigger picture of what God is doing: "Teach us to number our days, that we may gain a heart of wisdom" (Psalm 90:12).

We need to be intentional about taking time to reflect. We need to pause and consider what we've learned from our experiences, our successes, and our failures. We recognize where we need to grow, because who we are now is who we are becoming. As we take time to reflect, God gives us perspective, and shows us things that need to be shaped in us. We learn more about our default settings—ways we typically respond under stress—and learn also about different ways to respond.

The issue is one of preparation. Preparation increases the probability of a proper response in the heat of the moment when the pressure is on. Honest reflection leads us toward the kind of intentional character development that will keep us rooted in Jesus no matter what troubles come.

EXERCISE: PRACTICING REFLECTION

1. Set aside a specific time for reflection that is manageable for you (e.g., ten minutes every evening for a week, one Saturday morning for an hour).

2. Write that time down on your calendar and make sure nothing else crowds it out.

3. If necessary, find childcare or schedule your reflection for a time when children are sleeping.

4. Write down a few specific questions you can use to help you focus your reflection time. You might choose a few of the questions from this chapter that seem most relevant to you.

5. When the time for reflection comes, turn off your phone, computer, and TV, and go to a place where you are unlikely to be interrupted.

6. Begin your time by asking for God's guidance and presence.

Especially as we look to the past, it can be helpful to reflect together with others. Collective knowledge is greater than individual knowledge; a group will likely find a better approach than an individual. By talking with others, we can pool our knowledge and share our experiences, reflecting on strategies that have worked well in the past. In doing so, we are less likely to repeat the same mistakes as others. And we are more likely to try a different approach when it becomes apparent that our first approach isn't accomplishing what we want it to accomplish. Think, reflect, ask . . . and find out what works.

Once we have reflected on both our own lives and on God's larger plan, it is then time to stretch. We are to give ourselves to that which lasts, in whatever way God has designed us. We reflect, decide, then we risk. Not in foolhardy ways, but in ways that are thought out, prayed out, planned out—yet still a stretch.

PROVERBS:

✦ Proverbs 5:6: She gives no thought to the way of life; her paths wander aimlessly, but she does not know it.

✦ Proverbs 20:27: The human spirit is the lamp of the LORD that sheds light on one's inmost being.

CHECKPOINTS:

❏ Set aside regular time for reflection.

❏ Reflect both alone and by talking with others.

❏ Mine your past experiences for wisdom. What have you learned?

❏ Take stock of both your strengths and your weaknesses.

❏ Ask others for their perspectives and thoughts.

MANAGEMENT OF OUR EMOTIONS

We all have bad days. We all sometimes feel emotions like anger, worry, jealousy, or fear. That's normal. There is no such thing as good emotions or bad emotions. The key for us as followers of Jesus is to acknowledge whatever emotions we are feeling, and then decide how—and how not—to act on them.

Sometimes I (Tara) get stressed about money. Even in situations where things are pretty stable and most people wouldn't worry, I still will. I can feel my stress level rising if a bill is paid late or if an unexpected expense comes up. Once when I was in my twenties and still in school I discovered one April that I owed money on my taxes—and it was more than what I had in my bank account. So for a few days,

I panicked. Then after a while I realized that panicking was not help-ing matters, but actually making them worse. So I prayed, and then I figured out what kind of changes I needed to make so I could pay off my tax bill by the deadline.

We are in charge, not our emotions. Let's look at some simple ways that can play out in everyday life:

- ✤ Sonya does something kind, but does not receive kindness in return. She feels like lashing out at the other person's ingrati-tude with a sarcastic comment, but she chooses not to.

- ✤ Maria's teenage son is pushing her buttons. The kid seems to know exactly what to say to make his mother mad. Maria can feel her defenses rising, but chooses instead to give complete attention to her son and ask him what he needs.

- ✤ Two six-year-olds are arguing, and one yells back at the other, "You're not the boss of me!" and walks away.

- ✤ Isaac has always found his boss intimidating, but he gathers his courage to voice his opinion anyway.

Essentially, this practice is known as "individuation." You're in charge of yourself. Others can't *make* you feel a certain way. You can choose not to let others push your buttons; you can choose how to respond.

You can choose how to respond.

When emotions rise, we can choose. When we feel stress over whether or not someone will like us or not, we can choose not to waste energy worrying. It's wise to think through how we are coming across and how we can best serve that other person, but once we have done that we need to recognize that there's much we can't control. Therefore we live in an attitude of trust. Consider Jesus' words from the sermon on the mount:

Therefore I tell you, do not worry about your life, what you will eat or drink; or about your body, what you will wear. Is not life more important than food, and the body more impor-tant than clothes? Look at the birds of the air; they do not sow or reap or store away in barns, and yet your heavenly Father feeds them. Are you not much more valuable than they? Can any one of you by worrying add a single hour to your life?.... Therefore do not worry about tomorrow, for tomorrow will worry about itself. Each day has enough trouble of its own. (Matthew 6:25-27, 34)

The good news is that when we do feel off-center and have trouble managing our emotions, we can find help: through friends, through prayer, through support groups, through counseling, through coaching, and so on. We can find ways to connect with God in the moment and during stressful seasons. We can find the resources we need to stay centered in Christ in a way that leads us toward greater maturity. And we can give ourselves some grace. We are still created in the image of God, even when that image is not being expressed well. We always have the opportunity to repent, reconnect with God, and try again.

PROVERBS:

✦ Proverbs 29:22: An angry person stirs up dissension, and a hot-tempered person commits many sins.

✦ Proverbs 27:4: Anger is cruel and fury overwhelming, but who can stand before jealousy?

CHECKPOINTS:

❏ Make a list of your own personal hot-button issues that are most likely to knock you off-center. Ask a close friend to pray for you in one of these areas.

❏ Become more aware of situations where you feel out of control. Learn your default responses.

❏ Find resources that will help you manage your emotions, such as go-to scripture passages or a friend to call.

❏ When you begin to feel anger, worry, or fear, stop for a minute, breathe deeply, and pray.

LIFE BALANCE

As we follow Christ, we need internal stability and balance. We need consistent connections with him, regular deposits into our emotional/ spiritual accounts over time. Imagine a runner trying to run a marathon without having done any training beforehand. She would collapse well before the finish line. Consistent balance over time rather than cramming is what will get us where we want to go.

Likewise, we need an internal sense of balance in our lives to accomplish what we want. We'll need to decide what we want and then do what it takes to accomplish that—consistently over time. Ignoring distractions and not getting sidetracked, yet taking care of ourselves so we can continue moving toward our goal.

Our lives are made up of many parts: personal, emotional, relational, intellectual, physical, and spiritual. We need to take care of ourselves in all of these areas. Spending all your time serving is not the answer, spending all your time resting is not the answer, spending all your time studying is not the answer. We need balance in our lives: time spent with God, time spent with friends and family, time spent alone.

Balancing our lives is one of the most essential keys to staying centered. We need to make time for ourselves and take care of the inner person. We need to know ourselves well enough to know what we need—what is good for us and what is not. For example, different people will need different amounts of time alone. Different people will need different boundaries with the world.

Knowing ourselves and taking care of ourselves by creating a balanced life will allow us to stay centered in that which lasts: "And if what was transitory came with glory, how much greater is the glory of that which lasts! Therefore, since we have such a hope, we are very bold" (2 Corinthians 3:11-12).

LIVING A CHANGED LIFE

As we follow Jesus and grow in maturity, staying centered in who we are and who we are becoming, we live a changed life. We are not as we were before. The development of our character becomes increasingly Christlike.

> Follow God's example, therefore, as dearly loved children and walk in the way of love, just as Christ loved us and gave himself up for us as a fragrant offering and sacrifice to God.
>
> But among you there must not be even a hint of sexual immorality, or of any kind of impurity, or of greed, because these are

improper for the Lord's people. Nor should there be obscenity, foolish talk or coarse joking, which are out of place, but rather thanksgiving. For of this you can be sure: No immoral, impure or greedy person—such a person is an idolater—has any inheritance in the kingdom of Christ and of God. Let no one deceive you with empty words, for because of such things God's wrath comes on those who are disobedient. Therefore do not be partners with them.

For you were once darkness, but now you are light in the Lord. Live as children of light (for the fruit of the light consists in all goodness, righteousness and truth) and find out what pleases the Lord. Have nothing to do with the fruitless deeds of darkness, but rather expose them. It is shameful even to mention what the disobedient do in secret. But everything exposed by the light becomes visible—and everything that is illuminated becomes a light. This is why it is said:

Wake up, sleeper,
rise from the dead,
and Christ will shine on you.

Be very careful, then, how you live—not as unwise but as wise, making the most of every opportunity, because the days are evil. Therefore do not be foolish, but understand what the Lord's will is. Do not get drunk on wine, which leads to debauchery. Instead, be filled with the Spirit, speaking to one another with psalms, hymns and songs from the Spirit. Sing and make music from your heart to the Lord, always giving thanks to God the Father for everything, in the name of our Lord Jesus Christ. (Ephesians 5:1-20)

EXERCISE:

Read Ephesians 5:1-20 each day for a week, journaling about your response each time.

■ ■ ■

Isaac and Tasha had a big fight that night. She was angry, he came in with his defenses up, and the situation just escalated from there. Late that night, Isaac took a walk to cool off and thought about the evening. He decided the situation needed to change. And he decided that the change would need to start with  him. Even though he felt like her problems were worse than his, and even though he felt like she was being unfair, he committed to starting to work on his character and his own responses.

Isaac was close to his uncle, and next time he saw him, he told him about the situation and asked for prayer that he would change. He described his goal: he wanted to be able to stay centered even when Tasha was angry.

Even though the goal sounded simple, it was easier said than done. Isaac did lose his temper a few times, but through taking a few minutes to meditate in his car before coming into the house in the evening, he found he was able to stay centered more easily. He continued asking his uncle for prayer and began memorizing scripture that would help him refocus on his goal.

Over time, he found that as he made progress keeping his temper, Tasha seemed less angry. As she calmed down, Isaac then found it that much easier to keep his temper. One day he realized he enjoyed being home more than he used to. He found himself spending more time with Tasha and the twins.

As Isaac took stock of his life, he realized some re-prioritization was in order. He wanted to shift his life balance to include more family time and less work time. It took several months to make the needed changes at work, but Tasha supported his decision, which made it much easier. One year after that big argument, Isaac could look back and see a great deal of progress.

GROUP DISCUSSION QUESTIONS:

1. In what areas of your life do you have the most difficulty staying centered?
2. What is one thing you might do that could help in that area?
3. Describe the life balance you are currently living out in these areas: personal, emotional, relational, intellectual, physical, and spiritual.
4. Read over the passage at the end of the chapter, Ephesians 5:1-20. What stands out most to you?

SUGGESTED SCRIPTURE TO MEMORIZE:

Therefore everyone who hears these words of mine and puts them into practice is like a wise man who built his house on the rock. The rain came down, the streams rose, and the winds blew and beat against that house; yet it did not fall, because it had its foundation on the rock. (Matthew 7:24-25)

CHAPTER 4

Journeying with others

Isaac felt like his life was running in one big circle, from home to car to work to car and back home again. At work he had a demanding job in sales that required a lot of time and energy. At home he had a wife and twin three-year-old boys who seem to spend most of their waking hours running, hitting each other, and  making noise. And in the car, he had traffic. "It's really sad that sitting in traffic feels like the most restful part of my day," thought Isaac to himself at 7:00 am on the highway one morning.

While he drove, Isaac began to think about high school and the friends he had there. It seemed like he had so much more time then than he did now. How did that happen? And where were those friends now? How long had it been since he'd been out with a friend, just to have fun? He couldn't remember. He talked regularly with his uncle, but that was about it. His uncle was probably the only other person who really knew what was going on in his head.

And this was not a great time to be without friends either, thought Isaac. He was struggling with his marriage, his parenting, and his job. A bit more of a social network would be really nice, a group of people to talk with, to hang out with. But who? And even if he did have friends, when would he find the time to see them? Maybe this season of life just wasn't realistic for having friends and community. But now was precisely when he needed them most.

■ ■ ■

How many people do you know of who would say, "I have plenty of wonderful, supportive people in my life—no need for any more. Thanks, but no thanks!"

There may be some out there, of course. But for most of us, that's just not our reality. When we catch wind of these wonderful, supportive communities we sometimes suspect they are fictional—figments of our collective imagination.

Perfect communities are fictional.
But real communities are not.

It's certainly true that perfect communities are fictional. But real communities are not. They're flawed, but they're real and we need them. We cannot live the life of a disciple in isolation—we need others along with us.

> **And God seems to have designed it that way on purpose. It's rooted in our very nature as human beings created in the image of God. As we discussed in chapter one, God himself exists in trinity—in a constant state of relationship. Like him, we were created for relationship. We cannot follow him alone. We need others. Since creation, when God stated that it was not good for Adam to be alone, it's always been that way.**

Again I saw something meaningless under the sun: There was a man all alone; he had neither son nor brother. There was no end to his toil, yet his eyes were not content with his wealth. "For whom am I toiling," he asked, "and why am I depriving myself of enjoyment?" This too is meaningless—a miserable business! Two are better than one, because they have a good return for their labor: If they fall down, they can help each other up. But pity those who fall and have no one to help them up! Also, if two lie down together, they will keep warm. But how can one keep warm alone? Though one may be overpowered, two can defend themselves. A cord of three strands is not quickly broken. (Ecclesiastes 4:7-12)

THE NEED

We cannot follow God in isolation. We need to connect with others and journey alongside them. Yet most of us feel an internal sense of conflict about that. On the one hand, we desperately want community. On the other hand, we are desperately afraid of it. The fear and the need, the push and the pull. Like women—or men—can't live with 'em, can't live without 'em.

In the opening monologue of the film *About A Boy*, Hugh Grant's character talks about how he has insulated his life: "In my opinion, all men are islands. And what's more, now's the time to be one. This is an island age. A hundred years ago, you had to depend on other people. No one had TV or CDs or DVDs or videos or home espresso makers. Actually, they didn't have anything cool. Whereas now, you see, you can make yourself a little island paradise." Later, of course, he begins to feel the downsides of island life. Even with the messiness of involvement with other people's lives, he starts feeling the desire for that involvement.

Yet our independent island lifestyle continues to get in the way. Why do we lack community? What makes it difficult? Our western culture, a lack of time, too much money, too little money, urban anonymity, suburban isolation, rural remoteness, moving too frequently, being stuck in one place. The potential reasons are endless.

I (Tara) once visited a small fishing village in Italy. I went for a walk early in the morning. The buildings were planted close together with narrow walkways winding between them and up and down steep hills. When I came up over a rise, I saw five or six older women dressed in traditional clothes, gathered around a card table in a small square. Some were playing cards; others were standing up talking. Their families had lived in this village for generations and they had grown up together. And now there was this American tourist stumbling upon their open-air card game.

Not wanting to interrupt, I turned down another narrow street thinking how sad it was that we didn't have communities like this in the United States. Then a couple of months later, I stopped into a Denver McDonald's at 6:00 am on my way somewhere. There I saw four retired men sitting in a booth, coffee cups and newspaper strewn over the table, engaged in a spirited but friendly political argument.

Community can be almost anywhere when we start looking for it.

We can see it in small town cafes, where farmers gather for breakfast or coffee. We can see it on inner-city basketball courts. We now have virtual online gathering spaces, like social networking sites. Of course, we could spend all day on Facebook and still feel lonely, because we haven't been in the physical presence of other people. It's not the same. But when used well, technology can forge the initial connections through which we can go on to develop stronger community.

> *Community can be almost anywhere*
> *when we start looking for it.*

Some people really do feel they've exhausted their resources for finding community. They've joined things, they've started things. Nothing is working. That can be frustrating, and those frustrations are real. Certainly, community does not come easily. Sometimes we need to change our expectations—maybe this isn't the type of community I wanted or the environment I wanted it in, but it is something. Often we don't get community on our own terms.

And sometimes we just need to wait. For inexplicable reasons, God often has us walk through lonely seasons of life. So we wait, pray, and try to engage with others in a posture of openness. While waiting, we'll need to reflect on our own willingness to enter into community. Are we willing to be available to others, not just have them be available to us? Are we willing to invest in others, not just have them invest in us? Are we willing to pay the cost? Because there is a cost.

THE COST

Real community is messy, and deep down we know that. People are imperfect. We don't always get along. We feel superior or we feel inferior. We feel justified. We write each other off. We bail. We feel bailed on. The cost can be counted not only in time invested, but in pain experienced.

And sometimes the particular kind of pain we experience can bring back difficult parts of our own history. When someone raises their voice, we remember raised voices in our family growing up. Other people are one of the best ways we can see God. Yet our views of God have been damaged by negative interactions with others. We believe some of the lies and don't see ourselves properly.

I (Bob) once got a 98% on a test—the highest grade in the class—and my dad responded by asking me, "What did you miss?" The message I heard, even though unintentional, was that I'd never be enough. Less than perfection was not enough. We all have some of these types of messages in our lives, and they affect our relationships with others. Journeying alongside other followers of Jesus is our chance to reshape those beliefs and rethink the way we view God—and the way we believe he views us.

CHECKPOINTS:

Which of these enemies of community have you experienced?

- ❑ a spirit of self-sufficiency
- ❑ unwillingness to engage with conflict
- ❑ pretending we have it all together
- ❑ fear and mistrust

COMMUNITY WITH A PURPOSE

Relationships with other followers of Jesus that have the power and depth to shape us don't just happen. It would be nice to think they would just happen spontaneously, but that's not how it works. Unless we live in a communal type of situation where we see each other and engage with each other every day naturally, spontaneity isn't going to get us where we want to go. It's not enough. True community and relationships require effort on our part: investment, consistency, and intentionality.

> *True community and relationships*
> *require effort on our part.*

Community, once formed, isn't formed for its own sake. It's not just about having fun or having something to do on the weekends. Real community is formed for a greater purpose. It is a way of engaging with others in a meaningful way to move forward on the mission.

The group of people that comes together is not always based on personal affinity. Consider the cast of characters in the *Lord of the Rings* trilogy: they were all quite different—and did not always get along—but they came together around a common purpose: the destruction of the ring. Their journey together was not just being a group for the sake of being a group. They formed a group with a purpose, a mission, a common calling.

Likewise, we take up the calling of Christ, to live out the great commandment and the great commission. That is the larger purpose of a group of believers.

> # *Our purpose: the great commandment and the great commission.*

THE GREAT COMMANDMENT

Jesus replied: "'Love the Lord your God with all your heart and with all your soul and with all your mind.' This is the first and greatest commandment. And the second is like it: 'Love your neighbor as yourself.' All the Law and the Prophets hang on these two commandments." (Matthew 22:37-40)

THE GREAT COMMISSION

Then Jesus came to them and said, "All authority in heaven and on earth has been given to me. Therefore go and make disciples of all nations, baptizing them in the name of the Father and of the Son and of the Holy Spirit, and teaching them to obey everything I have commanded you. And surely I am with you always, to the very end of the age." (Matthew 22:18-20)

And while we are journeying on mission together, we find that we grow individually as well. It's as if the context of relationships gives the Holy Spirit a wider space in which to work. We are challenged and shaped and changed by the relationships that develop. We strengthen each other, support each other, challenge each other, and bring each other closer to God. We become better people because of those we journey alongside. And through the presence of God among us, we help them become better people too.

PROVERBS:

- ✤ Proverbs 27:17: As iron sharpens iron, so one person sharpens another.
- ✤ Proverbs 12:15: The way of fools seems right to them, but the wise listen to advice.

Given the purpose of a community of faith, choose your friends wisely. While we minister to all, those who support us in close relationships need to be people we can trust. Think through the qualities that are important to you. The qualities that matter will be different for each person, but some possibilities include trustworthiness, sensitivity to the Spirit, a heart of compassion, wisdom, not being prone to gossip, openness to change, and a willingness to challenge us when necessary.

Then look for those qualities in others—and develop them in yourself. Those are high standards. And no one is perfect, particularly not ourselves. So how can we go about becoming a better participant in a faith community? A good starting place is to consider the one-anothers found in scripture:

- ✤ Wash one another's feet
- ✤ Love one another
- ✤ Be devoted to one another
- ✤ Honor one another
- ✤ Live in harmony with one another
- ✤ Don't judge one another
- ✤ Edify one another
- ✤ Be in unity with one another
- ✤ Accept one another
- ✤ Instruct one another
- ✤ Wait for one another
- ✤ Have concern one for another
- ✤ Greet one another

✤ Serve one another

✤ Don't provoke or envy one another

✤ Bear one another's burden

✤ Show forbearance to one another in love

✤ Be kind to one another, forgiving each other

✤ Submit ourselves one to another

✤ Consider the other as better

✤ Be mindful of one another

✤ Don't lie to one another

✤ Bear with one another

✤ Forgive one another

✤ Teach and admonish one another

✤ Be at peace with one another

✤ Encourage one another

✤ Offer hospitality to one another

✤ Don't slander one another

✤ Confess our faults to one another

We are part of something bigger than ourselves. Others affect us and we affect others.

When an American couple moved to Germany a few years ago, they were surprised by the level of ownership their neighbors felt in maintaining a clean, well-maintained neighborhood. There's no need for homeowners' associations in Germany. Instead, the homeowner's association consists of your neighbors stopping by and mentioning that your flowers are looking a bit wilted or that some oil has leaked onto your driveway.

Sometimes we all need the
nudge of a neighbor.

The neighbors felt quite free to make these kinds of observations to the American couple. They were much less concerned about being rude than about keeping the whole neighborhood looking nice. After all, neglect impacts them too. In cases of proximity, those close to us are affected by us and have the right to speak into our lives if they see something that needs attention. Sometimes we all need the nudge of a neighbor saying, "Hey, your flowers are wilting. How about watering them?"

We need others who will not only challenge us, but who will help us—someone to help us pick up litter that blows along our street, someone to water the plants while we're away. We can't do it all on our own.

EXERCISE:

Read the passage below three times, slowly and out loud, meditating on its meaning.

> Therefore, as God's chosen people, holy and dearly loved, clothe yourselves with compassion, kindness, humility, gentleness and patience. Bear with each other and forgive one another if any of you has a grievance against someone. Forgive as the Lord forgave you. And over all these virtues put on love, which binds them all together in perfect unity. Let the peace of Christ rule in your hearts, since as members of one body you were called to peace. And be thankful. Let the message of Christ dwell among you richly as you teach and admonish one another with all wisdom through psalms, hymns and songs from the Spirit, singing to God with gratitude in your hearts. And whatever you do, whether in word or deed, do it all in the name of the Lord Jesus, giving thanks to God the Father through him. (Colossians 3:12-17)

If you're reading through this book alone, this is a chapter for you to take some extra time on. Think through some possible ways to build your community. Pray that God would show you the possibilities. Be willing to reach out to others, and be willing to ask for help. Sometimes relying on your community for help and support is the only way to move forward. And sometimes giving to your community is the only way to move forward. Other people provide both support for us and growth opportunities for us as we learn to love and serve them.

CHECKPOINTS:

Ways to build your community:

- ❏ Start an accountability group
- ❏ Join a small group
- ❏ Get a coach
- ❏ Join a ministry team
- ❏ Ask for help

Jesus calls us to a different kind of living—the life of a disciple. And we can't live that kind of life in isolation. We simply can't do it alone; we need others along with us. Developing a community around us can be a lot harder than it sounds. And it takes a lot longer than we might expect. But if we can just take those first few steps, we'll be moving in the right direction.

■ ■ ■

Later that day at work, Isaac found himself looking around his sales office. How many other people here might feel the same way he did? How many came to work, went home, then turned around and did it all over again the next day without any significant relational energy being poured into them?

Over the next couple of weeks, Isaac thought about what he wanted. He also talked with some other people in his office about what they wanted. And after all, these were the people he saw every day anyway. Why not start right here?

Eventually, Isaac asked three other men if they'd like to start meeting for coffee before work on Tuesday mornings. He asked men because part of what Isaac realized he wanted was a safe place where he could talk about some of the struggles in his marriage—and maybe even hear from some guys who had been there. Yet he recognized the contribution women could make too just by their unique perspective. Maybe he would try asking around the office a bit to find out what women want in their relationships. Certainly he'd never really understood that.

Isaac's plan was a simple one: they could each share what was going on in their lives, read a scripture passage, and then pray for one another. If they met early in the morning, Isaac explained, they wouldn't be needed at home. Stephen, Ezra, and SaVaun were all in, even though Stephen wasn't sure about the whole God part of it.

Stephen wasn't sure what he believed, but he was willing to go along for the ride and see what came of it. And he definitely felt the need for some men in his life, as he was facing the imminent birth of his first son. Stephen's own father had left when he was a baby, and he was feeling more than a little fear right now about becoming a father himself.

On that first Tuesday morning, Isaac was taken aback by some of the similarities in their lives. All were married with kids—or soon to have kids—and were struggling with feeling pulled in too many different directions: spend time with the kids, spend time with the wife, make money, build a career, fix stuff around the house that always seemed to be breaking.

Yet their personalities and natural default responses to the challenges in their lives were all quite different. By talking with each other, they were able to see some different options for handling the stresses of this stage of life. And by simply listening to one another they felt less alone.

This was only the beginning, of course. But it was a good beginning.

GROUP DISCUSSION QUESTIONS:

1. What do you need to change in your life to become a better friend and support to others?

2. In what ways have relationships let you down in the past? How can you approach them differently in the future?

3. What are some relationships already present in your daily life that you could work toward deepening?

4. How might you do that?

SUGGESTED SCRIPTURE FOR MEMORIZATION:

Two are better than one,
because they have a good return for their labor:

If they fall down,
they can help each other up.
But pity those who fall
and have no one to help them up!

Also, if two lie down together, they will keep warm.
But how can one keep warm alone?

Though one may be overpowered,
two can defend themselves.
A cord of three strands is not quickly broken.
(Ecclesiastes 4:9-12)

PART 2

Living Life: the day-to-day life of a disciple

In part 1 we've laid the foundation of being rooted and centered in Jesus. Now in part 2 we'll turn to how that centeredness helps us live as God's disciples in the world. Here we learn how to deal with many of the practical areas of life that can so easily trip us up. How we set our priorities, how we manage our time and our money, how we communicate with others, and how we deal with modern-day idols in our lives—all of these things have a major impact on our journey of following Jesus.

Remember that part 2, like parts 1 and 3, cycles back through the major areas of God, self and others—our three primary relationships. Each part of the book approaches these three primary relationships in slightly different ways.

Chapter 5: focusing priorities
We need to assess our responsibilities and listen to what God wants from us. Then we can decide what our priorities are and where we need to focus our energy.

Chapter 6: taking charge of life
We need to take responsibility for our own lives. How we spend our time and energy is up to us, including what we commit to doing and how we honor our word.

Chapter 7: playing well with others
We need to maintain good, clear relationships with others. This means communicating well, recognizing that all people are different, and resolving conflicts directly as they arise.

Chapter 8: *mastering money*

Our money is not our own—it belongs to God. We are stewards. Therefore, we need to be both responsible and generous with our money.

Chapter 9: *toppling idols*

We need to identify the idols in our lives, then we can strategically and intentionally move them out of our lives. Within that vacant space, we can then invite God to dwell.

CHAPTER 5

Focusing Priorities

Maria watched out the window as her thirteen-year-old son walked off with his friends. She did not like the kids he'd been hanging out with lately. Juan had always done well in school until this year, but now his grades were dropping. And he seemed to be getting into more trouble at school and in the neighborhood  too. Maybe this was just a normal part of the teenage years, Maria thought. But she couldn't help feeling like the friends Juan was spending his time with were contributing to this sudden shift.

Maria had made her opinions clear, of course. She'd never been one to hold back what she was thinking. But the more she pushed Juan, the more he retreated into his room and turned up the music. Her frustration level was rising.

Other areas of her life seemed to be going well. Maria loved her work with the midweek children's program at church, teaching at Sunday school, and her role in leading worship on Sundays. The ideas just flowed, although making them happen was a bit more challenging. That had always been her problem, Maria joked, too many great ideas and not enough time to make them all happen.

Maria was serving God. So why was Juan suddenly having these problems? And why was he not listening to her anymore? Maria had always tried her best to be a good parent—even when money was tight, even though she did not have the help of a husband. Wasn't God supposed to be honoring that now? That was the deal, right?

■ ■ ■

Life so seldom goes as we plan. And just when one area of life seems to be going well, another area starts falling apart. What has worked well for one season of life suddenly stops working. And it doesn't feel fair. Where is God in this? We thought we were following his will, doing what he wanted, and then suddenly the ground shifted. We are forced to stop and think. Which way were we supposed to be going again?

Life so seldom goes as we plan.

Wouldn't it be great if God spoke to each of us—out loud and early in our lives—and told us exactly what he wanted us to do? That way we could just keep moving in that same direction our whole lives and we would know precisely what we were aiming for.

But that is not how it works. It didn't even work that way for Abraham.

> By faith Abraham, when called to go to a place he would later receive as his inheritance, obeyed and went, even though he did not know where he was going. By faith he made his home in the promised land like a stranger in a foreign country; he lived in tents, as did Isaac and Jacob, who were heirs with him of the same promise. For he was looking forward to the city with foundations, whose architect and builder is God. (Heb. 11:8-10)

Did you notice the phrase "even though he did not know where he was going"? God said to go, but he didn't actually tell Abraham where. He just said to go. And Abraham spent a good deal of time in tents, wandering around in foreign lands, looking forward to a permanent home.

Most of the time, we can listen to God and get a general idea of what he wants us to do, but we don't always know exactly what that will look like or how to get there. And unexpected turns often surprise us along the way, encouraging us to turn back to God with a listening ear once more.

> That is the life of faith, not the life of sight. That is the life God calls us toward, a life we must discover as we go. And the starting point is where we are right now—wherever we are. We can begin now to focus our priorities and take steps in the direction we want to go.

PROVERBS:

✠ Proverbs 16:9: In their hearts human beings plan their course, but the LORD establishes their steps.

✠ Proverbs 25:2: It is the glory of God to conceal a matter; to search out a matter is the glory of kings.

THE PRESENT SITUATION

Let's run through the process of taking stock of our lives as they currently are. Start by considering existing responsibilities and important relationships. Do we have children? A spouse? Aging parents? Health limitations? Financial obligations? At different seasons of life, the answers to these questions may be quite different. But what are those answers right now?

Given our current situation in life, how can we best fulfill our responsibilities while still living as God has designed us to live? Sometimes it can feel like different aspects of our lives seem to be competing for our time and attention. When that happens, we will need to make choices.

Consider both the vision and the reality.

And to do that, we need to take the realities of our current situation into account. We may want giant oak trees, but if our yard is the size of a dog run we're not going to get too far—and we're certainly not going to get there tomorrow. We may want to grow a vineyard, but if we live in Wisconsin, the grapes won't grow there. We need to consider both the vision and the reality, then look for the points of connection between them. Those points of connection are where the opportunities lie.

One man studied music in school. He played with some bands for a while, but then got married and had kids. A friend of his from school is now touring with a band around the country. Sometimes this man feels a pang of jealousy and wonders what that lifestyle would be like. But he knows that he is right where God wants him to be at this season of life. He plays music occasionally around town, but recognizes that this isn't the season of life for a national tour.

OPPORTUNITIES

When we take stock of our lives, sometimes we see barriers. But if we look closely we can also see opportunities. Sometimes they appear to be just coincidences or circumstances. And they may be. But who knows if God placed them in our paths for just such a time as this. What we do with the opportunities that come our way matters.

Be very careful, then, how you live—not as unwise but as wise, making the most of every opportunity, because the days are evil. Therefore do not be foolish, but understand what the Lord's will is. (Ephesians 5:15-17).

How we live our daily lives matters a great deal. God expects us to use wisdom, to look for opportunities to do good, and to seek his will in all situations.

CHECKPOINTS:

❏ Given our life situation, gifts, and skills, how might God want to use us most?

QUESTIONS TO CONSIDER:

✤ What are my important relationships?

✤ What do those relationships require of me?

✤ What other responsibilities do I have (financial, past commitments, etc.)?

✤ What other limitations do I have (geographic, health, etc.)?

✤ What skills do I have? What gifts do I have? What resources do I have?

✤ How could I use those to glorify God and benefit others?

- ✤ What can I contribute that is unique?
- ✤ What opportunities do I have?

SAMPLE CONNECTIONS BETWEEN LIFE SITUATION AND OPPORTUNITIES:

- ✤ I have a large house near a college campus. It can be a safe house for students.
- ✤ I have a mother in a nearby Alzheimer's care facility. I could organize groups to go visit the residents once a month.
- ✤ I live on an isolated farm and am good with computers. I could organize an interactive blogging community on a subject I care about.

From there we embark on a journey of exploration.

HEARING FROM GOD

Every once in a while God speaks out of a burning bush (like he did to Moses) or comes to someone in a blinding light (like he did to Paul). But most of us find that's the exception rather than the rule. God doesn't generally spell out his will for our lives in advance in spectacular technicolor detail. We have to discover it, and usually that process is gradual. As we live and serve, we discover what we're good at and what gives us joy.

Then, as we are faithful and obedient to those parts of his will we do know, we will find out more and more as we go. We don't have to know the whole road—just the next step. As long as we remain faithful to loving God, loving others, and using the gifts and resources God has given us, we know we are heading in the right direction.

What that right direction actually looks like can be very different from person to person. We are each presented with different opportunities because of our circumstances and the people we know. Sometimes an opportunity falls into our lap—something that is good to do, but not something we would normally have sought out. A lost child presents himself on your doorstep. You change whatever plans you had that afternoon to make sure he gets safely home. "So then, if you know the good you ought to do and don't do it, you sin" (James 4:17). Sometimes the will of God is just common sense.

Yet other times, nothing obvious presents itself. In those cases, taking time to reflect and listen to God is essential. Pray, read scripture, talk with people you trust, do whatever you need to do to listen to God.

CHECKPOINTS:

Some ways to hear from God:

- ❏ listening prayer
- ❏ reading scripture
- ❏ asking others in your community what they see
- ❏ spiritual retreats
- ❏ paying attention to recurring thoughts
- ❏ acknowledging our desires
- ❏ try and see
- ❏ open doors/opportunities
- ❏ sensing a connection between a need and your abilities

PROVERBS:

- ✚ Proverbs 2:6: For the LORD gives wisdom; from his mouth come knowledge and understanding.
- ✚ Proverbs 9:10: The fear of the LORD is the beginning of wisdom, and knowledge of the Holy One is understanding.
- ✚ Proverbs 16:20: Those who give heed to instruction prosper, and blessed are those who trust in the LORD.

MAKING CHOICES

After hearing from God, we have some choices to make. We need to decide what strategic actions to take. When we make something a priority, we're not saying we're going to neglect everything else, but we do need to make room for this new priority. We'll need to stop doing or delay some other things in order to free up time and energy to devote to our priority issues.

That means making some choices. Often there are many good things to do, but we can't do them all. We need to decide. And we can't cram—most goals require regular investment. Consider health, relationships, spirituality, financial solvency. All of these things require steady effort over time. And for that, we need to make choices about how we spend our time and energy.

TAKING RISKS

Once we've thought through our responsibilities and opportunities, once we've listened for the voice of God and made some tough choices about our priorities, then we'll need to step out on faith. Like Peter stepping out of the boat to walk on the water toward Jesus, we also need to step out of the boat and onto the water.

Of course, we should remember what happened to Peter. He walked on water for a few steps, then felt afraid and began to sink. Steps of faith do involve risk of failure. There's no getting around that.

> Shortly before dawn Jesus went out to them, walking on the lake. When the disciples saw him walking on the lake, they were terrified. "It's a ghost," they said, and cried out in fear. But Jesus immediately said to them: "Take courage! It is I. Don't be afraid." "Lord, if it's you," Peter replied, "tell me to come to you on the water." "Come," he said. Then Peter got down out of the boat, walked on the water and came toward Jesus. But when he saw the wind, he was afraid and, beginning to sink, cried out, "Lord, save me!" Immediately Jesus reached out his hand and caught him. "You of little faith," he said, "why did you doubt?" And when they climbed into the boat, the wind died down. Then those who were in the boat worshiped him, saying, "Truly you are the Son of God." (Matthew 14:25-33)

Yes, Peter's faith did falter. But consider: he had enough faith to leave the boat in the first place. He didn't have to—it was his own idea, based on his faith in the power of Jesus. Fear and faith often go together, and we usually have a little of each. Even when our faith is incomplete, God honors the steps we take and doesn't abandon us when we falter: "Immediately Jesus reached out his hand and caught him." Even when we make some mistakes along the way, we are called to action. Throughout scripture, people take risks to obey God and demonstrate faith.

Although I (Tara) didn't sense that public speaking was going to be my life career, I did feel that for almost any type of leadership role, it would be important for me to become basically competent at talking in front of a group of people. I decided to make it a priority to learn, and one of those opportunities came in the form of teaching a class.

The first time I got up in front to speak, it went badly. I had prepared thoroughly and knew the material, but was so nervous that it made the students nervous for me. I was also mistaken for being a student at first, which didn't help my confidence level. But as the semester wore on, I slowly gained confidence and it ended up being a productive and helpful class. What starts off shaky doesn't have to end that way.

PROVERBS:

✦ Proverbs 17:3: The crucible for silver and the furnace for gold, but the LORD tests the heart.

FOCUSING PRIORITIES WITH THE FUTURE IN MIND

Deciding on our priorities is a matter of thought, discernment, and faith. We consider our responsibilities, listen to what God wants from us, then step forward with intentionality.

One dad came home tired after a particularly tough day at work. The whole drive home he'd been looking forward to sitting down on the couch and listening to some music before dinner. No sooner did he walk in the door than his six-year-old daughter bounded up, soccer ball in hand. "Daddy! Want to play with me in the yard?" This dad had already decided that spending time with his daughter was a very high priority. And although that didn't mean he was always available, he stopped and reflected that there may only be a few more years when she'd be so anxious to play and so desiring of his undivided attention. So he went outside with a smile on his face.

What can we be doing now that leads us toward the future we prefer? Many goals, like having a close relationship with our children when they are grown, require regular deposits over time. It can't be crammed. So we need to do what we can along the way.

We don't always know ahead of time where the steps we take will lead us. We hold our vision loosely, looking toward a future we cannot see, but we do take steps in that direction. And we trust that God will bring something good from that faithfulness.

Maria was talking with her friend Julie over coffee, complaining about Juan and the disrespectful way he had been acting. As she talked and Julie listened, Maria realized that what she was doing wasn't working. Even though she firmly believed Juan was at fault, Maria realized she needed a different strategy.  When she got angry with him, it just drove him further away from her and into his new crowd of friends. "Hmmm," she thought out loud. "But what other options are there? Do I just let him do whatever he wants?"

"What do you think he needs from you right now?" asked Julie.

"What?" asked Maria.

"I don't know," laughed Julie. "I don't have an answer! I was just asking what you thought."

"Oh. Well, I suppose we haven't spent as much time together as we used to. I've been so busy with work and other things."

"What other things?" asked Julie.

"All kinds of things," replied Maria. "Running the midweek kids' club, teaching Sunday school, leading worship."

"That's a lot."

Silence.

That *was* a lot, Maria realized. She loved starting new things and getting new ideas going. She loved all of the work she was doing at church. But maybe Juan needed her more right now than the church did. Maria decided on two new strategies:

One, she would delegate some of her work at church to other volunteers. She had gotten many of these new ideas started—maybe it was time to let some others do the work of keeping them going. Over the next month, she trained others to take over her roles with Sunday school and worship, keeping only the mid-week kids club, which took place on a night Juan was at soccer practice anyway.

Two, she would prioritize her time with Juan and be more intentional about talking with him. Instead of waiting until something went wrong and then yelling at him, she resolved to ask questions more, listen more, and not lose her temper. After all, what he was doing was his responsibility, not hers. He would face the consequences. She could just serve as a sounding board for him, mirroring back to him what was happening in his life.

For Maria, a step of faith was not doing some things. It was faith to believe that she and the world and the church would really be okay if she did *not* lead worship and teach Sunday school. It was faith to believe that God would not be mad at her. It was faith to believe that she could trust others to carry out those ministries. Instead, Maria felt she needed to refocus her priorities to give more time to her son. Her step of faith was not doing more at church, but doing less. She had come to the belief that that was what was needed in her life during this season.

EXERCISE:

Comment on Maria and Julie's interaction:

1. How would you describe the conversational style used by Julie?
2. How did Julie's approach avoid the defensiveness that can occur when personal perspectives are challenged?
3. How did Julie direct Maria toward Jesus?
4. How does Julie's approach compare or contrast to your own communication style in similar settings?

EXERCISE:

Rank your responsibilities in order of importance to you. If you are feeling overwhelmed, prayerfully consider what you might be able to delegate.

GROUP DISCUSSION QUESTIONS:

1. How would you assess your responsibilities in life?
2. What unique things do you have to contribute that God can use?
3. What opportunities do you see?
4. How do you best hear God's voice?
5. When you listen to God, what do you hear?
6. Where do you feel God calling you to a step of faith?
7. Where do you feel fear and faith in your own life?
8. How much do you believe God can really do?

SUGGESTED SCRIPTURE FOR MEMORIZATION:

Be very careful, then, how you live—not as unwise but as wise, making the most of every opportunity, because the days are evil. Therefore do not be foolish, but understand what the Lord's will is. (Ephesians 5:15-17).

CHAPTER 6

Taking charge of life

Maria ran through the doors of the church fifteen minutes late. Even after delegating many of her previous
roles at church, she still seemed to be running behind
all the time. Seems like offloading some responsibilities should have taken care of that problem—why
hadn't it? Well, she'd have to think about that later.

For now, Maria rushed down the stairs in time to find a few of the
teenage helpers milling around. The chairs were not set up for Kids'
Night; the lights in the classrooms were out. The children's pastor
would be here any minute. Maria ran around trying to get everything
set up. "Hey guys, can you lend a hand with these chairs?"

"I thought we were supposed to meet early to pray before Kids'
Night," said Ryan, a fifteen-year-old.

"Yeah, I was running late though. Traffic. We've got to get all this
stuff set up. Everyone else will be here in just a few minutes."

"Okay," said Lexi, thirteen, as she started setting up chairs. "Hey,
Maria, I made the play at school. Auditions were last week, and—"

Maria cut in, "We don't have time to talk right now. Let's talk after,
okay? We can catch up after the kids go home." Lexi looked doubtful,
but continued setting up chairs.

As people began trickling in, Maria exclaimed, "Oh, no! I still
have the art supplies in the car! Lexi and Ryan, can you help me carry

them in?" And they ran out to her car to try to find all the materials.

It turns out Maria had a great idea for an art project—the kids created a Bible story mural in the gym. They left happy and covered with paint. After the last of the kids were picked up, Ryan and Lexi helped Maria clean up.

"Wow, I sure am wiped out," said Maria, brushing her hair out of her eyes. "Glad everything went okay though. What was it you were going to tell me about beforehand, Lexi?"

"Oh, it's not a big deal. I'm going to be in a play at school."

"That's great—congratulations! I'd love to hear more about it sometime when we're not all wiped out! Well, see you next week then? And let's all try to get here at 6:00 pm next time so we can pray first, okay?"

■ ■ ■

Do you ever feel caught in rat race? Like you don't have time to do what you really want to do? "If I just had more time," we think. "If I could just get organized."

Ever feel caught in rat race?

Sometimes we feel like we're spending our whole life running from one thing to the next. We're overloaded, overwhelmed, spinning our wheels, and never doing what we really want to do.

We all feel that way sometimes. But when running around busy, late, stressed out, and distracted becomes the rule rather than the exception, then we really *do* have something to worry about. Surely there must be a way to live more sanely. But how?

Many people are surprised to find that the Bible doesn't address only "spiritual" issues but practical issues as well, giving us guidance about how we live our daily lives.

> We weren't created to be running around like chickens with our heads cut off. We were created to live at peace, centered in the Holy Spirit, with our eyes focused on the goal—even when the world around us is spinning. God has laid out a pattern in the scriptures for a different kind of living, a peaceful kind of living.

Let's stop briefly and look back at the path we've traveled in this book so far. We've recognized the ways we're created in the image of God. We're connecting with him and allowing him to shape our lives. We're journeying this path with others alongside of us, and doing our best to stay centered in the midst of the challenges of life. Given that foundation, we've prayerfully set our priorities based on what's important, committed to that direction, and begun taking the first steps in that direction.

But now, even though we've clarified our priorities and understand where we want to go, obstacles rise up to block us. We still have all of this stuff we have to do. How do we implement our priorities in the real world? How do we really live them out? It's not as simple as making a decision and then everything changes.

The goal of this chapter is to provide good, clear, practical ideas that we can take and use to help our priorities become reality.

MAKING AND KEEPING PROMISES

Promises, promises. It's all too easy to make promises left and right without much thought of having to make good on them. Yet Jesus taught that if we are people of our word, everything we say is a promise, whether we say "I promise" or not. There is no difference between saying "I will do X" and making a promise.

And do not swear by your head, for you cannot make even one hair white or black. Simply let your 'Yes' be 'Yes,' and your 'No,' 'No'; anything beyond this comes from the evil one. (Matthew 56:36-37, NIV)

If everything we say is a promise, then we need to think carefully before speaking and then commit to following through on what we have said we will do. If we do that consistently over time, we will gain reputations as people others can rely on. They will learn that they can trust us as they see us honor our commitments.

My (Tara's) daughter Chloe had just started preschool the previous month. One day, I was a few minutes late picking her up, and I found Chloe sitting on the bench in the school office. Chloe seemed okay, but was unusually quiet that afternoon. That evening, when my husband came home, she asked him, "Daddy, can you pick me up at school tomorrow?" What had seemed like a minor issue to the mother was a very big deal to the daughter. And it took many, many days of being on time at pick-up to reestablish trust.

Granted, we will all make mistakes sometimes. But as disciples of Jesus, we need to make sure we are known as people of our word—people whose yes means yes and whose no means no. In that way, we will stand out in a world of broken promises.

Checkpoints:

❏ Think of someone you've made a promise to that you've not yet fulfilled, and make it right this week.

Learning to say no

We need to say yes only to those things that we will really do, and no to all the rest. Saying no can be hard, but it's something we need to learn to do. If we are unable to say no, we are left feeling trapped into more obligations than we can realistically handle, and that's how we end up breaking promises.

Sometimes we need to say no even to good things, because we can't do everything. The key to that is discerning—and feeling confident in—what we sense God calling us to do. Take for example an issue of compassion for the poor. Do we sense that God wants us to serve the poor? Yes. That much is quite clear from scripture. But in what way does he want us to serve? Through our time? Through our money? Through the use of a particular kind of giftedness we have? And which poor does he want us to serve? Widows and orphans? Homeless men? Families in our inner cities? Refugees? The poor overseas? The answers to questions like these will differ from person to person as we each listen to the voice of the Spirit.

In the end, we'll have to say no to some commitments. And saying no can be hard. What if people don't like us? What if we look unspiritual? What if we are being selfish?

A man was asking his pastor about the church partnering with a particular community organization that was important to him. He truly viewed it as a great opportunity for the church and couldn't understand why the pastor didn't want to do it. "Doesn't Jesus matter here anymore?" he asked in frustration. The pastor could feel himself starting to lose his temper, but instead responded calmly and firmly, "Yes, Jesus matters here. But you are not Jesus."

> ## *The only person responsible for the commitments we make is ourselves.*

God calls us all to different commitments and it is up to each one of us to discern what he has for us, rather than being pressured by others into being a part of something else. Remember that the only person responsible for the commitments we make is ourselves.

If we think through what we really want to do and what we really believe in, then giving an answer one way or another—and sticking to it—can be freeing. Knowing what we are about and what we are not about gives our lives a focus and a sense of purpose.

COUNTING THE COST

In order to be able to follow through on our promises, we need to think through what we commit to. Before we say either yes or no, we need to count the cost.

> Suppose one of you wants to build a tower. Won't you first sit down and estimate the cost to see if you have enough money to complete it? For if you lay the foundation and are not able to finish it, everyone who sees it will ridicule you, saying, 'This person began to build and wasn't able to finish.' (Luke 14:28-30).

Saying yes to too many things ensures we won't have enough resources to finish any of our projects well. Saying no to everything ensures that we build nothing. Both are equally unhelpful places to be.

Because I (Bob) am a visionary, I tend to commit to too many things. After all, there are so many great ideas to pursue. So in recent years, I've been growing in becoming more careful about what I commit to. And when I do commit to something, I check to make sure I'll have enough resources and time to be able to accomplish it. Last year this new approach led me to take a sabbatical from my teaching responsibilities to focus on a new church I'm planting. As everyone who knows me can attest, that's serious growth for me!

It's like the old saying, "Don't bite off more than you can chew." If we want to plant a garden, we need to decide how much garden we can commit to. Maybe it's best to start with a window box instead of an acre. If the window box goes well, then maybe we move on to a small vegetable patch in the back. And so on, as we see how much we are able to commit to caring for and nurturing. Sometimes we need to start with just a window box—but we do need to start somewhere.

SEEING PROJECTS THROUGH TO COMPLETION

Making promises—the right promises—is the beginning. Following them through to completion takes us the rest of the way there. The apostle Paul agreed:

> And here is my judgment about what is best for you in this matter. Last year you were the first not only to give but also to have the desire to do so. Now finish the work, so that your eager willingness to do it may be matched by your completion of it, according to your means. For if the willingness is there, the gift is acceptable according to what one has, not according to what one does not have. (2 Corinthians 8:10-12)

If we over-commit, we're not going to be able to follow through. We are to complete what we commit to. Sometimes that means we must engage in the mundane, day-to-day work of taking care of responsibilities. Planting a garden is one thing. Tending it and watering it, consistently and over a long period of time, is quite another. That part can be boring or tiring or can be forgotten all together. Yet those consistent investments are necessary for its growth. When we undertake a project, we need to be the kind of people who will see it through to the end. We need to decide to do the work and then do it, watering regularly, fertilizing regularly—even when we don't feel like doing it.

PROVERBS:

- ✦ Proverbs 12:22: The LORD detests lying lips, but he delights in people who are trustworthy.
- ✦ Proverbs 16:3: Commit to the LORD whatever you do, and he will establish your plans.
- ✦ Proverbs 20:25: It is a trap to dedicate something rashly and only later to consider one's vows.

TAKING TIME TO PLAN

It's a good practice to take a few minutes every morning—or the night before, for those of us who are night people—to look at the day. We can check to see what appointments we have, identify the things we need to get done, then rank them in order of importance. Once a week, we can take a step back to look at the whole week to see the bigger picture. What do we need to get done this week? In the same way, we can make a list, put it in order of priority, and then spread it out strategically over the week. We can choose to set a series of appointments, or blocks of time, so that they reflect our priorities.

Even things that don't always seem like appointments to us can be scheduled in this way: time with God, time with our kids, time to work out, projects at work. We can carve out time by proactively scheduling space in our calendar that reflects our priorities. Then when people come to us and ask for something, we can look at our calendar and see whether we have a previous commitment. That commitment may be to spend time with God, but if it reflects our priorities, we should honor it as a previous commitment. This approach allows us not to have our lives dictated by the tyranny of the moment, but rather by what God has shown us we need to put first.

When we begin feeling frazzled with too many things to do, that's a signal to slow down and plan. Slowing down can seem counterintuitive when we feel overwhelmed, but it's actually the best time to stop and prioritize what's most important. If the engine light begins blinking on your dashboard, it means something is wrong. Our natural tendency is to smash the light or cover it up to make it go away, while we keep on driving so we can get just a little further on our trip. But that light is a signal that we should stop and deal with the underlying problem.

MAKING AND KEEPING APPOINTMENTS

Making and keeping appointments is like making and keeping promises: we need to do it according to our priorities and we need to recognize that we can't do everything. Even those of us who prefer to do a little bit of everything can't do it all at once.

There is a time for everything,
and a season for every activity under the heavens:

a time to be born and a time to die,
a time to plant and a time to uproot,

a time to kill and a time to heal,
a time to tear down and a time to build,

a time to weep and a time to laugh,
a time to mourn and a time to dance,

a time to scatter stones and a time to gather them,
a time to embrace and a time to refrain,

a time to search and a time to give up,
a time to keep and a time to throw away,

a time to tear and a time to mend,
a time to be silent and a time to speak,

a time to love and a time to hate,
a time for war and a time for peace.

What do workers gain from their toil? I have seen the burden God has laid on the human race. He has made everything beautiful in its time. He has also set eternity in the human heart; yet no one can fathom what God has done from beginning to end. (Ecclesiastes 3:1-11)

There is always enough time to do God's will.

There is an appropriate time for everything. We each have only twenty-four hours in a day, and we need to decide what activities are important enough to spend those hours on. Then we need to decide in what order to spend them. These skills are known as prioritizing (deciding what's important) and managing (figuring how to best spend your time each day).

There is always enough time to do God's will. God will never give us more to do than we are able to do. When we feel overwhelmed, we can stop and ask ourselves what we believe God's will is—for us, right now. God is not asking the impossible. Therefore, what is God's will for us today? What can be done later, by another person, or not at all? Usually when we look at it that way, we come out re-centered with a fresh perspective.

PLAN FOR THE UNEXPECTED

As life gets busier, we may need to schedule things further in advance. Yet we'll need to build in some flexibility by leaving enough margin. Essentially we need to plan for the unexpected. As a rule of thumb, it can be helpful to leave two hours a day that are unscheduled. That's as true for busy businesspeople as it is for young mothers. We'll need that time for the surprises that are bound to happen. If we schedule our lives completely full, then what happens when the car breaks down, when we get an urgent phone call from a friend, when the baby gets sick?

When we fill our schedules too full with commitments, then we're stressed when the unexpected comes (and it usually does). Remember there is always enough time to do God's will. So leave some room for those "divine appointments."

All of this means taking a look at the bigger picture, prioritizing what's most important to us, then scheduling it in, but leaving ourselves some margin for the unexpected. That way, we'll get the essentials done, but we'll also need to be realistic enough to release the stuff that just isn't going to happen.

DAILY TIME MANAGEMENT

Finding the appropriate time is a matter of assessment, sensitivity to the Holy Spirit, prioritization, organization—and then living it out.

Step 1: Assess: What are my responsiilities?

Step 2: Discern: What do I sense the Holy Spirit putting on my heart?

Step 3: Prioritize: Which activities are more important?

Step 4: Organize: Which activities would it be best to do when?

A little forethought goes a long way. Prioritizing and managing our time can be as simple as organizing the following daily activities:

✤ Today I have to go to the grocery store and I have to pick the kids up from school at 3:00 pm. Since the grocery store and the school are right near each other, maybe I should go to the grocery store either right before or right after I pick up the kids. That way I only make one trip, saving both time and gas.

✤ Today at work I have one-hour meetings at 9:00 am and 11:00 am, several quick phone calls to make, email to check, and one large project to work on that will take some concentration. If I check email first thing in the morning, then make all my phone calls during that hour between meetings, that leaves my whole afternoon free to focus on the big project.

✤ I have to arrive for my shift at work at noon. The three things I would like to do this morning are getting a haircut, going to the bank, and cleaning my apartment. I don't have time to do all three before noon. I need to choose between cleaning my apartment and running the two errands. Whichever I don't do this morning, I can do tomorrow morning before work.

RUNNING LATE

Running late is one of the most common symptoms of lack of time management. Often it results from the lack of advance planning discussed above. Sometimes there are deeper reasons in play.

A man had a month where he was consistently running late. Once, after yet another meeting that he'd joined late, this man's ministry partner took him aside and said, "Do you realize what statement you're making when you're late? You're saying that there is absolutely no one in this world who is more important than you are and everyone can wait for you."

Another common reason for consistently running late is that we keep trying to do that "one more thing" before we leave. When I (Bob) was in college, my mentor once told me, "You're not late because you didn't run fast enough. You're late because you didn't start early enough." He was right. And really, why not start earlier and risk arriving a bit early? Now I bring something along to read, socialize before an event, or just be quiet and enjoy the moment when I arrive early.

CHECKPOINTS:

Problem > Solution

❏ running late > don't try to cram in too much right before you have to be somewhere. Or start getting ready earlier. Leave in time to arrive a few minutes early.

❏ forgetting appointments > keep and use a calendar. Check it every day.

❏ canceling at the last minute > make a contingency plan for emergencies

❏ no-shows > if you absolutely cannot make an appointment, call to cancel. Letting others know shows respect for their time.

❏ missing deadlines > do foundational work well in advance so things have time to simmer. Then you'll just be putting on the final touches right beforehand.

❏ forgetting to take care of things you said you'd do > When you commit to doing something, put a reminder on your calendar two days before it needs to be done to jog your memory.

PROVERBS:

✛ Proverbs 20:4: Sluggards do not plow in season; so at harvest time they look but find nothing.

✛ Proverbs 24:27: Put your outdoor work in order and get your fields ready; after that, build your house.

✛ Ecclesiastes 11:4: Whoever watches the wind will not plant; whoever looks at the clouds will not reap.

CHECKPOINTS:

❏ Plan ahead.

❏ Leave yourself more time than you should need.

❏ Keep and use a calendar.

❏ Call if you are going to be late or absent.

SIMPLIFY AND FOCUS

Some of us may be feeling rather discouraged right about now. This can all seem like quite a lot to absorb, let alone do. And it is, especially when so much of it is rooted in the habits of our daily lives. So start small. We don't have to change everything all at once. Choose one or two things to try and start doing them regularly. See what a difference it makes. Yes, these can be difficult patterns to change. But the freedom we gain if we do is worth it.

I (Bob) recently went through my library and purged about 60% of my books by selecting the ones I wasn't using anymore and giving them away. I also went through my files and reduced them by about 50%. Although it's hardly my default to go through my office and clean it out, I decided to do it during the writing of this book and found that it did create a lot more freedom and space.

First things first, one thing at a time, always one more thing.

One of the best ways to start simplifying is by doing one thing at a time. Remember this maxim: "First things first, one thing at a time, always one more thing." After prioritizing (first things first), then focus (one thing at a time). There's a lot of talk in our culture about the benefits of multitasking, but we don't really do all that well with it. We were wired to only be able to give our full focus and concentration to one thing at a time. We can't really engage with our child and be reading the newspaper at the same time. We can't really talk on phone and grocery shop at the same time—unless we don't mind coming home without half the items we meant to pick up. Divided attention results in doing both things poorly, slowing us down rather than speeding things up.

DISCOVER WHAT WORKS FOR YOU

Certainly, some of the skills in this chapter come more naturally to some people than to others. But the key is knowing yourself and knowing what works for you.

One man who had to give presentations at work found that his most productive time for developing the material was the day before. It felt current and fresh to him that way, and he was energized by the approaching deadline. After years of feeling bad about his preparation style, trying to prepare in advance and ending up doing it over again at the last minute anyway, he finally decided to try a different approach.

He would do the pre-work in advance: reading, thinking, sifting through the information. He would also—well in advance—block out the day before the presentation as a time to put it all together. And for him, that strategy worked well. The material felt fresher, he spent less time overall preparing, and he came away with a better presentation.

If morning prayer doesn't work well for you and finds you falling asleep on God, stop feeling guilty. Instead, set aside time to pray in the evening or in the afternoon. Feeling bad doesn't help. Changing our approach does.

Feeling bad doesn't help.

We should each spend our time doing what is most productive for us. Each plant has a limited amount of energy. If some branches are not thriving, we can prune them to conserve our energy for the healthy branches—those that are working. "I am the true vine, and my Father is the gardener. He cuts off every branch in me that bears no fruit, while every branch that does bear fruit he prunes so that it will be even more fruitful" (John 15:1-2).

No one can do everything. So why spend our time on what isn't working anyway? If that area is something we truly value, we can find another approach that will work.

CHECKPOINTS:

- ❏ Identify areas in your life that aren't working.
- ❏ Are they important or unimportant?
- ❏ If something important isn't working, find a different way to do it.
- ❏ If something unimportant isn't working, stop doing it.
- ❏ If managing your time and commitments is an area of challenge for you, get a coach or an accountability partner and list out specific things you'd like to work on.
- ❏ Don't try to change everything at once. Choose just a few items at a time.
- ❏ Give yourself some grace—it takes time for new habits to form.

Taking responsibility for our lives matters. We can make our own decisions about the way we choose to live. Although it doesn't always feel that way, how we spend our time and energy is up to us.

■ ■ ■

When Maria met with the children's pastor later that week, she told him she didn't like how Kids' Night went. Although it seemed like a success on the surface, she just didn't feel good about it. A few questions from the pastor unleashed an avalanche of words from Maria. She told him about being late, about how  tired she felt after scrambling around looking for the art supplies, about feeling like she wasn't investing enough in the teenage helpers, about feeling like she had missed some opportunities to talk with them and pray with them. "I know there are all kinds of more things I should be doing."

"Maria, it doesn't sound to me like you should be doing more. After all, you just cut some responsibilities from your schedule, and that was a good thing. Don't work more—just work smarter."

"I hear that kind of thing and I never know what it's supposed to mean!" Maria's voice was edged with frustration.

"Sorry. All I mean is that it sounds like you could use some help organizing your time a bit better. You've already decided on your priorities. Now you just need some help translating those choices into your day-to-day life. Think about it this way—Jesus was never in a hurry. He had a whole lot to do, but he did only one thing at a time, and he focused on just that one thing. Whenever he talked with someone, he was fully present. And because he was human, and had the same twenty-four hours in a day that we have, there were plenty of things he didn't do. He didn't heal everyone. He didn't talk to everyone. He didn't invest in one hundred disciples. There just wasn't time to do it all. So he picked and chose, but what he did he did well."

Maria went home and thought it over. She prayed, and tried to hear the Spirit's voice in all of this. As she thought and prayed, she realized that she was living in a constant state of crisis—always on a deadline, running on adrenaline, prepared with ready-made excuses for things not being right. She was tired of living that way.

The next day she called the children's pastor. Together, they went over some strategies for helping her organize her time. She committed to limiting TV to one hour a day in her home. Among other things, that freed up half an hour in the morning that she could use to think through her day and make a list of the essentials that she needed to get done that day. If other items fit into that list, great. If not, they'd have to be dealt with later.

So the following week, instead of trying to cram in the vacuuming right before leaving for Kids' Night, Maria let it slide. She left early and was at the church, ready to pray, when Ryan and Lexi showed up. After Kids' Night, she made an appointment with Lexi to get together later in the week—because she wanted to hear more about the play and what else was going on in her life. And she wrote it down on her calendar, with a half hour of buffer time blocked out beforehand.

GROUP DISCUSSION QUESTIONS:

1. In what areas of my life have I overcommitted?
2. In what areas of my life have I avoided committing?
3. What are some of my fears around commitment?
4. In what relationships has my *yes* not been *yes* or my *no* not been *no*?
5. Thinking of my current commitments, which of them did I count the cost for beforehand? Which did I not?

SUGGESTED SCRIPTURE FOR MEMORIZATION:

And do not swear by your head, for you cannot make even one hair white or black. Simply let your 'Yes' be 'Yes,' and your 'No,' 'No'; anything beyond this comes from the evil one. (Matthew 5:36-37, NIV)

CHAPTER 7

Playing well with others

Today was the day Harry had been dreading. Today he began the ninth step of his recovery: making amends. Although many of the earlier steps had been painful too, this was the one he had been especially dreading. While working on the eighth step—making a list of all the people he had harmed—so many faces had  come to mind. Some of them he hadn't seen in quite a long time. Some of them he knew very well.

His ex-wife, who never missed an opportunity to tell him what a deadbeat lowlife he was. His daughter in college, who thought she was so much better than her unemployed father. His son in the Navy, who blamed Harry for all his problems.

At least these were the ways Harry had gotten used to thinking of his family. Now that he had taken responsibility for more of his life and now that he had met Jesus, he understood that some of those beliefs weren't strictly accurate.

But he still dreaded talking with any of his family members.

Harry went to talk with his small group leader about it. Steve was a really down-to-earth kind of guy, as Harry saw it. Even though Steve had never done the twelve steps himself, he would probably get it, Harry suspected. He would understand.

When Harry finished telling Steve about his fears about moving into the ninth step, Steve looked surprised. "That's the ninth step?

Making amends to those we've harmed? Wow, it's like they stole the idea directly from Jesus. I wonder if they did." Then he went on to tell Harry what Jesus said in Matthew 5:23-24: "Therefore, if you are offering your gift at the altar and there remember that your brother or sister has something against you, leave your gift there in front of the altar. First go and be reconciled to that person; then come and offer your gift."

"Making amends—reconciliation—has been a Christian tradition for a long time," explained Steve. "Easier said than done, of course. But Jesus knew we couldn't really worship the Father or live freely until we had done what we could to try to make things right with others."

"That makes sense," said Harry, his downcast eyes staring at the table between them. "But it's still going to be pretty hard. And I sure don't expect warm, forgiving responses."

■ ■ ■

We would all like good, clear relationships. Wouldn't that be nice? After all, what does every parent want to see on their child's first report card? "Plays well with others." That's because we know that's often a good predictor of how happy and successful that child may be later in life. Junior may not be able to count to ten yet, but if he can get along well with others we breathe a sigh of relief.

But unfortunately, good, clear relationships with those around us are not the present reality for many of us. Often we have a history of broken relationships in our past—people we would rather not see or people who would rather not see us. It's not always possible to fully repair those damaged relationships. But it is possible to try to mend them. And it is possible to adopt new ways of relating with others that will help us be less likely to damage our relationships in the future.

That's what we're going to look at here: new ways of communicating with others that will result in healthier relationships. To create and maintain good, clear relationships, we'll need to work on listening, responding in truth and grace, resolving conflicts, avoiding gossip, and recognizing that others may be different from us.

LISTENING

James, the brother of Jesus, gives us the golden rule of communication: "My dear brothers and sisters, take note of this: Everyone should be quick to listen, slow to speak and slow to become angry" (James 1:19).

- ✤ Quick to listen
- ✤ Slow to speak
- ✤ Slow to become angry

It's stunning how much trouble we could keep ourselves out of by following these three simple rules. But just because they're simple doesn't mean they're easy. Simple and easy are two different things.

Simple and easy are two different things.

Seeking to truly understand another person is hard work; it takes time and patience. But many communication issues can be resolved if we take the time to understand what the other person is trying to say rather than jumping to conclusions. Sometimes we react too quickly, assuming we understand someone's meaning. As Proverbs says, "To answer before listening—that is folly and shame" (Prov. 18:13).

One of the most common core problems in communication is not understanding what the other person is trying to say. We too often listen selectively, camping on a word or two, and then jump to a conclusion. We want to evaluate what the other person is saying—deciding if it's right or wrong—before we've really heard it. So we end up telling people they're wrong before we've taken the time to listen. The discipline is to hear what the other person is truly trying to say. If we take the time to understand, we're much less likely to jump to conclusions.

Asking good questions is our best ally as we try to understand others. The use of open-ended questions is essential. The best questions begin with "what" or "how" and cannot be answered with yes or no. Questions like this are much less likely to meet with a defensive response—and much more likely to get at the roots of another person's meaning.

Another problem in listening arises when we try to interpret what the other person is saying. We interrupt and try to finish their sentences for them. "Here's what you meant to say. Here's what you're trying to say." In this way, we put our own spin on what they are trying to communicate and try to fill in their meaning for them. Rather than putting ourselves in the middle of it, we need to take the time to unpack what they're saying by listening and asking questions.

Of course, all of this is easier said than done. This is really tough stuff, especially when the other person is saying something that might be difficult, painful, or sensitive. In those cases, not reacting to what we think we're hearing is hard. It requires staying centered and rooted in Christ. But when we do it, the reward is that the other person knows we've heard them. When we have listened well enough to be able to reflect back to them what they're trying to communicate—to their satisfaction—they feel heard. And that goes a long way.

A while back I (Bob) got looped into conversation with a couple of Mormon missionaries. Normally, I try to avoid that situation, as it only serves to sharpen their training, but in this case I needed to engage. I spent an hour and a half seeking to understand their concept of God. After that, I was able to articulate to their satisfaction their understanding of who God is.

At that point, I moved to respond. "So I've taken the time to understand who God is from your perspective. After an hour and half I'm now able to articulate clearly and accurately your view of God. It would only be fair for you now to hear my understanding of God." They said, "Oh, that's easy!" and then proceeded to get it all wrong. I had to go by that time, so I asked to set up a second meeting.

The following week, they brought the head of their local church's education program, along with a host of other missionaries. I came prepared to take a look at a hundred different verses that show Jesus is God. I had only gone through the first three and they didn't have answers for them. So I said, "I have dozens more passages, and if any of you are really interested in looking at this with me, I'd be happy to talk with you one-on-one if you have the courage." The head of the education program later became a believer and was baptized. And one of the things that led to that point was me taking the time to fully understand what they were saying. Doing that shows respect for the other person even if you strongly disagree with them.

Here's the basic principle: Before responding, unpack the other person's position fully so you can verbalize to their satisfaction what they're trying to say. One benefit of this approach is that it gives the other person the chance to refine their meaning. As they hear us—without us evaluating or interpreting—repeat back to them what they're saying, sometimes they hear their own words and think, "That's not quite right." It helps them refine their communication and make midcourse corrections, and it allows them to sharpen their expression and retract what they didn't really mean. That helps us too. If we stay grounded, we can help them get to that point, but if we react, that helps nothing.

Before responding, unpack the other person's position fully.

Especially if we are feeling attacked or don't like what we think another person is saying, we need to slow down. Instead of reacting, we need to clarify what the other person actually means. "Here's what I'm hearing you say....Is that what you mean?"

This strategy alone often resolves the miscommunication. Many times the other person will say, "That's not what I intended to say," or "I didn't mean it like that." Now of course, not all situations require that we go to this level of depth, but practicing this skill can avoid many of the misunderstandings that result in conflict and separation.

Most people, given the opportunity to correct themselves, realize they weren't clearly communicating and that what they said had an unintended meaning. And if they don't correct themselves, at least both you and the other person will be clear on the intention. One sports coach made a statement to a reporter that the reporter knew would be controversial. Before it went to print, she read back to him what he had said, and asked, "Are you sure you want to go on record saying this? I'm giving you a chance to revise your statement." He refused to revise his statement, and it became a big problem in his career.

As followers of Jesus, we can show grace to others by giving them a chance to correct or clarify what they've said before it "goes on record." After all, who among us has not misspoken or said something that had an unintended meaning? In being quick to listen and slow to speak, we give others the benefit of the doubt and the chance to be heard more clearly. And only after we have listened and understood do we move on toward speaking.

RESPONDING IN TRUTH AND GRACE

Most of us tend to err on the side of truth or grace. We may respond in truth, but in a way that is hurtful. Or we may respond in grace, but we hedge in such a way that we're not helpful. The best way is not balancing the two, but being filled with both: "Instead, speaking the truth in love, we will in all things grow up into him who is the head, that is, Christ" (Ephesians 4:15).

Think before speaking.

One good tip for learning to respond well is to stop and think before speaking. It's helpful to take a few minutes to organize our thinking and decide what key things are most important to say. Narrow it down to just two or three key items—don't try to communicate too much at once. Organizing our thinking beforehand rather than speaking off the cuff takes some effort, but it helps a great deal and we get better at it over time.

Once we know what we want to say, we can then try to say it in the most helpful way possible. Avoid using polarizing phrases such as "always" and "never." After all, how well do we like it when someone says to us, "You never help out around the house!" or "You're always late!" Another way to communicate well is to use "I messages" rather than "you messages." Instead of saying, "You were unkind when you said X the other day," we could say, "I felt hurt when you said X the other day." It may seem like a subtle difference, but usually the hearer responds much better to "I statements" than to "you statements."

Once we've said what we want to say, ask, "What do you hear me saying?" If we just say something and assume the other person's got it, they may walk away thinking something completely different. Summarize what the other person is saying and then ask them to summarize what you're saying.

RESOLVING CONFLICTS

If we practice these principles—listening, clarifying, summarizing, thinking before we respond, speaking in truth and love—we will avoid a lot of conflict. However, some conflict is an inevitable part of living in community with others. Since we are all imperfect, when we get together, conflict is inevitable. The good news is that working through conflict well can strengthen community rather than destroying it. Jesus laid out a clear process for dealing with conflict:

> If a brother or sister sins, go and point out the fault, just between the two of you. If they listen to you, you have won them over. But if they will not listen, take one or two others along, so that 'every matter may be established by the testimony of two or three witnesses.' If they still refuse to listen, tell it to the church; and if they refuse to listen even to the church, treat them as you would a pagan or a tax collector. (Matthew 18:15-17)

A clear progression is set forth in this passage. And the first step in that progression is to go and talk directly to the person concerned, just between the two of you. The combination of directness and kindness is a powerful one.

Conflict is inevitable.

CHECKPOINTS:

When addressing conflict, do so in the following ways:

- ✜ with an attitude of prayer
- ✜ face-to-face and in-person
- ✜ with a willingness to listen
- ✜ remaining present and calm (resisting the fight-or-flight temptation)
- ✜ recognizing that the conflict may not be resolved, but knowing that you are doing everything you can in good conscience
- ✜ with an openness to mediation if necessary

Always go directly to the source. When you pull weeds, you need to pull out the roots, not just the tops. If you only pull out the top, the weed just grows right back again—sometimes even faster, as if it's just been pruned. In the same way, if you're trying to address conflict without going directly to the person you're in conflict with, the problem is going to just keep cropping up, and usually in worse and worse ways.

Always go directly to the source.

The apostle Paul sets this example for us in his conflict with Peter (Cephas): "When Cephas came to Antioch, I opposed him *to his face*, because he stood condemned" (Galatians 2:11, emphasis added). Always go directly to the other person involved in the conflict. Anything less is counterproductive. It's like treating the symptoms of a disease without addressing the cause. It's like pulling off the top of the weed but leaving the roots intact. Always go for the roots.

CHECKPOINT:

Think of someone you are in conflict with, reflecting on the questions below. Make a list of possible next steps you could take to move toward reconciliation. Pray over them. What do you sense God calling you to do?

- ❏ How have you attempted to resolve the conflict up to now?
- ❏ How has the other person attempted to resolve the conflict?
- ❏ How much discomfort are you willing to face to define the real problem behind the conflict?
- ❏ How have you discussed your feelings with this other person in the conflict?
- ❏ How have you contributed to the escalation of this problem?
- ❏ What would you most like to see happen as a result of addressing this conflict?
- ❏ What are you most interested in gaining?
- ❏ What is the other person most interested in gaining?

PROVERBS:

- ✜ Proverbs 26:18-19: Like a maniac shooting flaming arrows of death is one who deceives a neighbor and says, "I was only joking!"
- ✜ Proverbs 26:21: As charcoal to embers and as wood to fire, so is

a quarrelsome person for kindling strife.

✜ Proverbs 21:9: Better to live on a corner of the roof than share a house with a quarrelsome wife.[3]

AVOIDING GOSSIP

Gossip is one of the most underestimated sins in the church today. Gossip does far more damage than many other behaviors churches are quick to focus on. It has the power to tear communities apart like nothing else.

Gossip is one of the most underestimated sins in the church today.

Gossip is passing along information to people who aren't a part of the problem or a part of the solution. Gossip is especially damaging when the information is personal and/or negative. A good street definition: talking about somebody behind their back. And for those in churches, remember that gossip in the form of a prayer request is still gossip.

Proverbs is filled with condemnations of gossip:

✜ Proverbs 20:19: A gossip betrays a confidence; so avoid anyone who talks too much.

✜ Proverbs 26:20: Without wood a fire goes out; without a gossip a quarrel dies down.

✜ Proverbs 26:22: The words of a gossip are like choice morsels; they go down to the inmost parts.

One good strategy for combating gossip is to refuse to receive it. When someone begins sharing something about another person, stop them early and ask, "Have you gone to so-and-so and talked with them directly?" If the answer is no, let them know you don't want to hear any more until they've gone to the person concerned and tried to resolve the situation. If everyone responded that way, gossip would stop. If the person is too afraid to do that, then offer to go with them and help

---

[3] Although not directly mentioned in the proverb, sharing a house with a quarrelsome husband is not much fun either.

facilitate the discussion. Gossip is a profoundly damaging behavior, and refusing to receive it goes a long way towards bringing healing.

Sometimes people gossip because they're being malicious. Sometimes they just want to be seen as interesting. Other times people share (a common Christian synonym for gossip) indirectly because they're afraid of talking with the person directly. Fear prevents us from initiating difficult conversations, being honest about how we feel, and asking the hard questions. Sometimes when we're afraid, it just seems easier to avoid the problem. And fear also makes us much more likely to put our energy into defending ourselves rather than listening and trying to understand others. Fear is a primary enemy of good communication.

> ### *Fear is a primary enemy of good communication.*

Whether we are the offended or the offender, whether we are angry at someone else or they are angry at us, we'll need to have the courage to take initiative and go to them directly. "Therefore, if you are offering your gift at the altar and there remember that your brother or sister has something against you, leave your gift there in front of the altar. First go and be reconciled to that person; then come and offer your gift" (Matthew 5:23-24). Whether the matter is someone else's fault or our own—or most likely, some of each—it's our responsibility to do what we can to resolve the problem. "If it is possible, as far as it depends on you, live at peace with everyone" (Romans 12:18).

RECOGNIZING THAT OTHERS ARE DIFFERENT FROM US

Living at peace with people who are different from us presents certain challenges. We all have different personalities. Some of us are more expressive, while others are more reserved. Some of us are more serious, while others are more lighthearted.

We all have different needs. Some of us feel powerfully the need to be liked. Others would much prefer to be respected. Some feel the need for independence, while others want inclusion. And we feel these different needs to varying degrees.

And on top of all this, we tend to deal with communication and conflict in different ways. In any given relationship or conversation, when tensions rise, we have different defaults.

For example:

✤ When you feel a conflict arising, do you feel the temptation to run or to fight?

✤ When you feel attacked, is your most immediate response to defend, to retreat, or to counterattack?

✤ Do you more often feel the need to make peace or the need to be right?

The point is simply this: not everyone is like you. Take into account that others may be acting out of very different needs and desires than you would in their position. People are different—some need a bit of space, others may need more engagement. When communicating or when in conflict, take into account who the other person is. What do they want? What do they fear? What do they need?

Not everyone is like you.

Even in simple situations, our needs are not always the same as the needs of others. Once I (Tara) was at the home of an acquaintance when she got an unexpected phone call with some bad news. She started crying and was very upset. I immediately felt that I should make a quick and polite exit. After all, this woman didn't know me very well and probably wanted to be rid of company just then. If the tables were turned, I certainly would have wanted her to go. But as it turns out, this other woman wasn't me, and she insisted I stay. She wasn't just being polite—she really wanted company in her distress. In fact, having me leave just then would probably have made her feel even worse.

Sensitivity to the Spirit and to the cues of others is essential. Good communication isn't easy for any of us. But Jesus calls us to do what we can to maintain good, clear, honest relationships with others. That means communicating well and clearly, recognizing that all people are different, and working to resolve conflicts directly so we can move toward unity and reconciliation. By our love and our unity, others will most clearly see the work of Jesus here on earth. Remember Jesus' prayer before his disciples in John 17:20-23:

My prayer is not for them alone. I pray also for those who will believe in me through their message, that all of them may be one, Father, just as you are in me and I am in you. May they also be in us so that the world may believe that you have sent me. I have given them the glory that you gave me, that they may be one as we are one— I in them and you in me—so that they may be brought to complete unity. Then the world will know that you sent me and have loved them even as you have loved me.

■ ■ ■

For the next three weeks, Harry dragged himself out of bed every morning with fear in his heart. He prayed to God, trying to center himself for these difficult conversations. He tried to get himself to a place where he could communicate without blaming, where he could take responsibility for his actions, and where he could  be direct without losing his temper. Harry prayed each morning until he felt like he could listen without defending himself. Some days it took a really long time. Then one afternoon he picked up the phone to call his son.

Mike was in the Navy and stationed overseas. Harry knew he wouldn't be able to talk with Mike in person for quite a few months, but he felt he should at least start the process now in whatever way he could. After several missed connections, he finally reached Mike. Mike sounded okay, but a little hesitant, as if afraid his dad was calling to ask for money again.

With Mike's permission, Harry launched into his story. He talked about being off drugs for nine months now, about his new relationship with Jesus, and about his desire to make things right with Mike. He apologized for much of the past. Then, with a deep breath, he asked Mike how that sounded to him. Mike paused for a full 30 seconds, which felt really long.

"Well," Mike began, "you've apologized before and I'm not sure why I should believe you this time. But this does sound a bit different to me. You're not trying to make me see how hard it is for you, not trying to gain my sympathy. It almost sounds like you're taking responsibility."

They talked for almost an hour, and it was a rough conversation at times, but Mike agreed to meet with his dad in person next time he was on leave. And he ended the conversation by saying, "You know, Dad, this is something I've wanted to hear from you for a really long time. I'm not sure if I can trust it, but I want to try."

All in all, much better than Harry had expected.

After taking a couple of days to recover, Harry tried calling his daughter. Lisa refused to meet with him, asking why she should waste her time. Harry said that he understood her anger and that if she ever wanted to tell him more about it, he'd be glad to listen, apologize, and try to make things right. Then Lisa swore at him and hung up the phone.

The following week, Harry walked into a diner to meet Peggy, his ex-wife. He was early. As he sat there waiting, he began to wonder if she would really show up. She did. And she immediately launched into a tirade against him. It was the kind of tirade that only people who have been together for years—and have been fighting for years—can truly understand. With each sentence, the grooves in this well-traveled road got a little bit deeper and a little bit more entrenched. He had heard much of this before. Why did she have to keep repeating herself?

Harry felt his anger and defensiveness rising. His usual responses to her usual accusations rose quickly to his mind. But he stopped and asked himself the question he had prepared beforehand: "What will happen if I say that?" He knew exactly what would happen—they'd have the exact same argument they'd been having for years. Harry knew it by heart and didn't want to have it again. It was like watching a bad rerun over and over again. So he tried to think of something different to say.

The only thing that came to mind sounded a bit lame to him, but he said it anyway: "Tell me more." Peggy looked at him stunned, and for a few seconds was at a loss for words. But not for long. She started again. Then when she began running out of fuel, he asked her, "What has this been like for you?" Asking that question after being harangued for half an hour was one of the hardest things Harry had ever done. After all, no one was asking him what this was like for him. No one cared.

Forcing his attention back off himself and onto Peggy, he tried to make himself listen. It was over an hour before she asked him anything about himself. And when he had his opportunity, Harry wanted so badly for her to understand how hard this had been for him. But he resisted and instead shared his sorrow over the pain he had caused her and their children. She looked at him with furrowed eyebrows, not sure what to think. Then she burst into tears.

After those conversations, Harry felt a load lifting from his shoulders. Sure, Lisa was still unwilling to talk with him, but he felt like he had done what he could to leave that door open. He hoped that someday it might make a difference to her that he had at least tried. And he looked forward to seeing Mike again soon. And who knew where things would go with Peggy—she wasn't sure what to think yet.

As Harry sat down in his apartment that night to listen to some music, it was a bittersweet celebration, but a celebration nonetheless.

GROUP DISCUSSION QUESTIONS:

1. Of the following challenges, which is the most difficult for you?
   - Having the courage to be direct
   - Having the courage to be honest
   - Having the courage to be vulnerable
   - Having the courage to listen without defending
   - Having the courage to initiate hard conversations
   - Having the courage to ask the hard questions
   - Having the courage to put others first

2. Think of someone you are or have been in conflict with. What are some of the ways you've allowed fear, selfishness or gossip to enter into those relationships?

3. What is your own default way of handling conflict? What might you do to grow in this area?

4. Who do you need to talk with?

SUGGESTED SCRIPTURE FOR MEMORIZATION:

My dear brothers and sisters, take note of this: Everyone should be quick to listen, slow to speak and slow to become angry. (James 1:19)

CHAPTER 8

Mastering Money

Sonya sat at the desk in her apartment, paying bills. This was easily one of her least-favorite activities. It always made her feel small somehow—limited and boxed-in. Nothing extra left over at the end of the month. How did other people manage to get savings?

Everyone always said going to college would help her get a good job, which would then provide a comfortable living. Sonya felt more like college had just left her with a giant student loan to pay off. Although she liked her job teaching social studies at the public high school, it did not provide her with much more than what she needed to pay her bills and the student loan.

Sonya had really expected to be married by now. Surely that would have solved her financial problems, she thought. But at thirty-seven, she was wondering if marriage was really in the cards for her. She felt disappointed and left to make it on her own—both relationally and financially. This was not plan A.

So whenever Sonya had felt like splurging on something, she either charged it or stopped by the ATM. She didn't keep track of those extra purchases at first—they seemed rare, more the exception than the rule. But over the past few years they had become more regular. And about six months ago she had been surprised to find a credit card balance she couldn't pay. More and more of her credit card payment started going toward the interest.

Every once in a while, Sonya's brother Raymond would call her to ask for money. Raymond struggled with mental illness. When he was on his medication, he could hold down a job. But whenever he went off his medication, he ended up losing that job. And the first person he called was Sonya. Sonya always gave him whatever she could—usually enough to get him back on his feet in the short-term.

Between Raymond's most recent call and Sonya's credit card debt, she found herself unable to pay her monthly bills. So Sonya decided to cut back on her giving. It was just for now, she told herself. Just until she got things straightened out financially. Since her early twenties, Sonya had been giving regularly to the church and to the local rescue mission and she liked being able to do that.

But after a couple of months of feeling unable to give, Sonya's discomfort rose to the point that she was willing to ask for help getting her finances in order. But who should she ask?

■ ■ ■

Money may not seem like a very spiritual topic. What does money have to do with following Jesus? Money is for this world, not the next. That may be true, but Jesus is for both this world *and* the next. And he had a whole lot to say about money. Listen to this parable Jesus told:

> Do not store up for yourselves treasures on earth, where moth and rust destroy, and where thieves break in and steal. But store up for yourselves treasures in heaven, where moth and rust do not destroy, and where thieves do not break in and steal. For where your treasure is, there your heart will be also.…No one can serve two masters. Either you will hate the one and love the other, or you will be devoted to the one and despise the other. You cannot serve both God and Money. (Matthew 6:19-24)

In fact, money—including issues like poverty, wealth, greed, and generosity—is one of the most commonly addressed themes throughout the Bible. Far from considering such matters beneath our spirituality, God seems to have a good deal for us to hear and learn about money. And it's a hard area for us to grow in.

> The way we think about and handle money finds its roots deep in our core. Either we master money or it masters us. As Jesus said, "For where your treasure is, there your heart will be also." Changing our hearts so we can live responsibly and generously can be hard. Habits and beliefs will both need to change, and that will not come without hard work, prayer, and the intervention of the Holy Spirit in our lives.

Yet the rewards are great. As Billy Graham once said, "If a person gets his or her attitude toward money straight, it will help straighten out almost every other area of life."

WHOSE MONEY IS IT?

One of the biggest lies we believe about our money is that it is ours. In reality, our money is not our own—it belongs to the Lord. We are managers. This is the first shift we need to make in the way we think about money.

By thinking of money as our own, to do whatever we choose, we create an idol. An idol is something we look to for security, status, or comfort instead of God. We'll talk more about idols in the next chapter. But one thing about idols: they give us the illusion of control, and then they turn on us.

Idols give us the illusion of control.

They can never quite deliver the security, status, or comfort they pretend to offer.

Listen to this parable Jesus told:

Then he said to them, "Watch out! Be on your guard against all kinds of greed; life does not consist in an abundance of possessions." And he told them this parable: "The ground of a certain rich man yielded an abundant harvest. He thought to himself, 'What shall I do? I have no place to store my crops.' Then he said, 'This is what I'll do. I will tear down my barns and build bigger ones, and there I will store my surplus grain. And I'll say to myself, 'You have plenty of grain laid up for many years. Take life easy; eat, drink and be merry.' But God said to him, 'You fool!' This very night your life will be demanded from you. Then who will get what you have prepared for yourself?' This is how it will be with those who store up things for themselves but are not rich toward God." (Luke 12:15-21)

Our money is not our money— it belongs to God.

As we release our grasp on money and recognize it as a temporary blessing—entrusted to us for a time, but really coming from the Lord and still belonging to him—we are freed from idolatry. Our money is not our money—it belongs to God. We are only managers, entrusted to use it well and invest it wisely for the short time we have it under our control:

Again, it will be like a man going on a journey, who called his servants and entrusted his wealth to them. To one he gave five bags of gold, to another two bags, and to another one bag, each according to his ability. Then he went on his journey. The man who had received five bags of gold went at once and put his money to work and gained five bags more. So also, the one with two bags of gold gained two more. But the man who had received one bag went off, dug a hole in the ground and hid his master's money. (Matthew 25:14-18)

Money and spirituality cannot be separated. The way we handle money has a great impact on our spiritual life as well. As Jesus said, "So if you have not been trustworthy in handling worldly wealth, who will trust you with true riches?" (Luke 16:11). So how should we become trustworthy in handling worldly wealth?

Money and spirituality cannot be separated.

EXERCISE:

Read the whole parable of the talents (Matthew 25:14-30) and discuss the following principles of money management found there:

- ✦ God owns it all (v. 14)
- ✦ We are in a growth process (v. 21)
- ✦ The amount is not important (v. 23)
- ✦ Faith requires action (v. 27)

PROVERBS:

- ✦ Proverbs 30:7-9: Two things I ask of you, LORD; do not refuse me before I die: Keep falsehood and lies far from me; give me neither poverty nor riches, but give me only my daily bread. Otherwise, I may have too much and disown you and say, "Who is the LORD?" Or I may become poor and steal, and so dishonor the name of my God.

- ✦ Proverbs 15:16: Better a little with the fear of the LORD than great wealth with turmoil.

- ✦ Ecclesiastes 5:10: Those who love money never have enough; those who love wealth are never satisfied with their income.

- ✦ Ecclesiastes 4:5-6: Fools fold their hands and ruin themselves. Better one handful with tranquility than two handfuls with toil and chasing after the wind.

CONTENTMENT: LIFE THAT IS TRULY LIFE

"Who is rich? He who rejoices in his portion."

—rabbinic proverb

The first step toward handling our worldly wealth well is a shift in attitude and perspective. Most of us, no matter how much money we have, feel like we need just a little bit more. As we shift our attitude around money, we need to come instead to a place of contentment with what we have. Our true wealth is not here on earth anyway, but in heaven (see again Matthew 6:19-24, quoted above). Once we really understand that, once we give up worrying over our money and trying to protect it, we can come nearer to contentment:

But godliness with contentment is great gain. For we brought nothing into the world, and we can take nothing out of it. But if we have food and clothing, we will be content with that. Those who want to get rich fall into temptation and a trap and into many foolish and harmful desires that plunge people into ruin and destruction. For the love of money is a root of all kinds of evil. Some people, eager for money, have wandered from the faith and pierced themselves with many griefs. (1 Timothy 6:6-10)

We begin to fully understand that the riches of this world are temporary, while God is eternal. As we live accordingly, we "take hold of the life that is truly life":

Command those who are rich in this present world not to be arrogant nor to put their hope in wealth, which is so uncertain, but to put their hope in God, who richly provides us with everything for our enjoyment. Command them to do good, to be rich in good deeds, and to be generous and willing to share. In this way, they will lay up treasure for themselves as a firm foundation for the coming age, so that they may take hold of the life that is truly life. (1 Timothy 6:17-19)

> *He doesn't want us to live our lives in pursuit of that which doesn't matter.*

The vast majority of us reading this book would be considered "rich in this present world." If I have a roof over my head and know where my next meal is coming from, I'm rich in this present world. But don't worry—God cares about the rich too. He doesn't want us to live our lives in pursuit of that which doesn't matter. He wants us to take hold of the life that is truly life. To do that, we need to have our hands free and open—recognizing that God is the true owner of our money.

MONEY MANAGEMENT AND SAVINGS

"Getting money is like digging with a needle. Spending it is like water soaking into sand."—Japanese proverb

As we look toward the nuts and bolts of how to manage our money effectively, we must begin with two essential commitments. One is the commitment to obey God, whatever that requires of us. That's a significant step of faith.

The other commitment is tracking where our money goes. We cannot manage what we cannot find. We must know where our money is going before we can become intentional about how to best use it. Before creating a budget or plan, take a month and simply track where all of your money is going. Write down everything you spend; itemize credit card statements; keep your checkbook current. Once you know how much you are spending on what, you can decide where to make adjustments.

The basic road map for financial success is to learn to spend less than what we earn. If we can do that for a long time, we will be financially stable. A good rule of thumb is the 10/70/20 rule. First we honor God by giving away 10 percent of our income. Then we meet our obligation to the government through paying our taxes (Luke 20:22-25). After that, here's what we do with what's left:

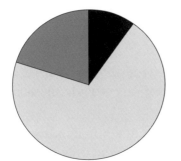

10% of our income goes into long-term savings (i.e., retirement)

70% of our income goes toward living expenses (mortgage/rent, food, utilities, insurance, etc.)

20% of our income goes toward paying off our debts or toward a savings account for emergencies

Using this system ensures that we have money in reserve for those times when the car breaks down. And long-term savings creates compounding interest, which leads to financial security. "Dishonest money dwindles away, but whoever gathers money little by little makes it grow" (Proverbs 13:11).

One of the benefits of coauthoring a book—as opposed to writing it all by yourself—is that you get to be challenged by another person's ideas. I (Tara) had written a full draft of this chapter, was pretty happy with it, and sent it off to Bob. Bob said, "I like all the stuff that's in there—our money belongs to God, generous giving, tracking expenses and budgeting—but we'll need to add a section on saving." Saving? Oops . . . I'd conveniently forgotten that part.

So if you're feeling discouraged right about now, don't worry— everybody has something to work on. It's a matter of starting wherever we are. And to figure out where we are, we need to start keeping track of where our money is going.

I (Bob) began using an envelope system with my wife Janet right after we got married. When I got my paycheck cashed (no direct deposit back then), I'd get small bills and we'd put them in different envelopes for food, gas, entertainment, etc. We had seven dollars a month ear-marked for clothing, and it took me almost a year to save up enough for a new pair of shoes. The soles of my shoes had holes in them, so I just made sure the soles stayed on the ground when I was in meetings. When I had saved enough for a new pair, I asked the salesman to rec-ommend a type that would last. I came out of the store with a pair of wingtips, and they became a symbol to me of living within my means and not overspending. Next time I had to buy a pair of shoes, I got wingtips again even though they had long since gone out of style. In fact, they probably weren't in style the first time I bought them.

CHECKPOINTS:

Tips for mastering money:

❑ Don't be afraid to ask for financial advice when you need it. Many churches and nonprofit organizations provide financial planning advice.

❑ Take on only "good debt." Student loans and home mortgages (when taken out in reasonable amounts) are the only types of debt with a potential upside. Car payments and credit card debts leave you paying interest for items that are losing value rather than gaining value.

❑ Don't buy anything on credit that you don't have a plan for paying off.

❑ Identify some non-essential areas where you've been spend-ing money (e.g. going to restaurants instead of cooking, new clothes that could wait, extra gas money for non-essential trips) and cut those out temporarily.

❑ Go cash-only for a while. Cash-only means using cash or checks or money orders—no credit cards. Cash-only allows you to more easily track what you spend, and it doesn't allow you to spend what you don't have.

❏ Start saving in advance for big expenses you know will be coming (e.g., when you know you'll need to replace an aging car or computer soon).

❏ Delay gratification. This means living within what you can afford right now rather than what you would like to be able to afford someday.

EXERCISES:

✦ For one month, write down everything you spend, down to the dollar. At the end of the month, organize the expenses by category (groceries, gas, restaurants, etc.). What trends do you notice?

✦ Create a budget. Put income in one column and expenses in the other, making sure expenses are lower than income. What would it take to live this budget out consistently?

Generous giving has never been about the amount—it's always been about the heart.

GENEROUS GIVING

When my wife and I (Bob) were serving as missionaries, the ten-year-old daughter of one of our investors wrote us a letter: "I've included twenty-seven dollars here to help with your ministry. I've saved it out of my allowance, prayed about who to give it to, and wanted to give it to you." This is a child on track toward being a generous giver.

Generous giving has never been about the amount—it's always been about the heart.

Jesus sat down opposite the place where the offerings were put and watched the crowd putting their money into the temple treasury. Many rich people threw in large amounts. But a poor widow came and put in two very small copper coins, worth only a fraction of a penny. Calling his disciples to him, Jesus said, "Truly I tell you, this poor widow has put more into the treasury than all the others. They all gave out of their wealth; but she, out of her poverty, put in everything—all she had to live on." (Mark 12:41-44)

Generous giving stems from the certainty that God will provide for our needs. God tells us that he will provide for us.

"Bring the whole tithe into the storehouse, that there may be food in my house. Test me in this," says the LORD Almighty, "and see if I will not throw open the floodgates of heaven and pour out so much blessing that there will not be room enough to store it. I will prevent pests from devouring your crops, and the vines in your fields will not drop their fruit before it is ripe," says the LORD Almighty. "Then all the nations will call you blessed, for yours will be a delightful land," says the LORD Almighty. (Malachi 3:10-12)

A trust that God will provide for our needs frees us to loosen our grasp on our money and give from a heart of generosity. Generous giving starts at ten percent (often called a tithe). Ten percent is the amount the Israelites in the Old Testament were commanded to give, and we are at least as blessed as the average Israelite.

Generous giving can be hard at first. How can we move toward obeying God in this area? There are two approaches: diving in and wading in. Some people take the plunge, take the leap of faith, and just start doing it. Others begin their giving at 2 percent, then increase it in six months to 4 percent, so that by the end of two years' time, they'd be giving a tithe.

Giving reminds us of where our priorities lie.

I (Tara) decided to dive in. Actually, my husband made me dive in, but I agreed to go along. When we decided to start tithing, I was still in school, working part-time, and my husband was making about nine dollars an hour. When we figured out ten percent for the month it came to one hundred dollars. One hundred dollars! That was quite a lot of money—and I wouldn't be getting anything at all for it. That was a hard check to write.

But giving is like exercise. If we do it regularly, it gets easier. And just as exercise prevents the build-up of toxins in our bodies and keeps everything in good working condition, regular giving prevents greed from taking over, from corrupting our hearts and enslaving us. Giving reminds us of where our priorities lie. There is a certain sense of inner peace and joy that comes from knowing that your actions are consistent with the deeper desires of your heart.

> Suppose a brother or sister is without clothes and daily food. If one of you says to them, "Go in peace; keep warm and well fed," but does nothing about their physical needs, what good is it? In the same way, faith by itself, if it is not accompanied by action, is dead. (James 2:15-17)

> If any one of you has material possessions and sees a brother or sister in need but has no pity on them, how can the love of God be in you? Dear children, let us not love with words or tongue but with actions and in truth. (1 John 3:17-18)

As we meet the needs of others, we take hold of the life that is truly life. And we are freed. And we realize that it's not only others and the kingdom of God that benefit by our giving. We benefit. Generous giving helps with our own faith development, and it's one of the clearest ways we can express Jesus' lordship in our lives. And the generous spirit we develop in the way we approach others returns to us. "Give, and it will be given to you. A good measure, pressed down, shaken together and running over, will be poured into your lap. For with the measure you use, it will be measured to you" (Luke 6:38).

PROVERBS:

- ✦ Proverbs 3:9-10: Honor the LORD with your wealth, with the firstfruits of all your crops; then your barns will be filled to overflowing, and your vats will brim over with new wine.

- ✦ Proverbs 28:27: Those who give to the poor will lack nothing, but those who close their eyes to them receive many curses.

- ✦ Proverbs 22:9: The generous will themselves be blessed, for they share their food with the poor.

We can't serve both God and money. By refusing to give to God, we are in fact serving money. Something powerfully spiritual happens to us as we give, and it releases us from money's mastery over us.

Changing the way we handle our money can completely transform the rest of our lives. One couple ran into financial trouble and, upon tracking where their money was going, they realized with a shock that they were spending exactly twice as much as they were making. They were willing to make some major changes in their lifestyle and take drastic steps. They cut up their credit cards and called the credit card companies to alert them. They dramatically reduced their expenses and spending, and began paying down their debt. At the very same time, they started to give away ten percent of their income.

> *Changing the way we handle our money can*
> *completely transform the rest of our lives.*

It was trial by fire, and it took a long time, but after three years this couple had completely paid off their debt. They had worked hard at tracking their expenses, disciplining their spending, and honoring God with their money. Their spiritual lives took off, and they were now financially freed to be able to take positions teaching overseas, which was something they would certainly have been unable to do with the burden of their previous debt. Their lives were changed.

Managing our money well—being both responsible and generous—requires a lot of effort and hard work. But it can be done and God helps us as we trust in him and move forward.

CHECKPOINTS:

Steps to get out of debt

❏ Commit your money to God. Determine that with God's help you'll get out of debt.

❏ Cut up your credit cards. (Alternately, you could also preheat the oven to 400 degrees and bake them for 10 minutes to produce credit card kringle.)

❏ List what you owe, and to whom. Contact all of your creditors and honestly relate your problem.

❏ Designate 20 percent of your net income to paying off debt.

Pay a little toward each debt, but pay the most on those with the highest interest rates.

❏ Buy on a cash basis only.

❏ Sacrifice your wants until your debts are paid.

■ ■ ■

Sonya knew she was in over her head, but she had no idea who to call. She still hadn't figured it out when she met for coffee the next day with her team leader for the neighborhood service project she was involved in. The team leader told her about a financial adviser who did seminars on money management. However, these seminars were not free. The financial advisor charged a sliding scale fee based on each person's ability to pay.

Sonya was frustrated. A seminar to help you get back on your feet financially—but it still costs money! However, she recognized she was stuck, so she grudgingly decided to sign up anyway and pay the thirty dollars. On the first evening, the presenter explained that anything you value must come with a price of some kind. Money is connected with what we value. That's why he charged a sliding scale fee for the seminar: so people would value the advice and be more likely to act on it. He added that the regular price was two hundred dollars.

The rest of the seminar included both practical advice (similar to that given earlier in this chapter) and general principles. For example, Sonya learned that every time she spent money she did it for a reason—and sometimes that reason went deeper than she had thought. When she went out to treat herself to a new outfit, it wasn't just because she needed a new outfit. The purchase fueled a deeper, unstated belief that this new outfit would help her attract a husband, which would in turn fill her needs and give her worth and value. When she thought about it at a conscious level, the idea seemed silly. Yet she felt a pang of inner certainty that this belief did indeed lay beneath many of her clothing purchases.

As Sonya started thinking through the reasons behind her spending, she was able to sort out which areas could be cut back on (e.g., clothing) and which things could remain (e.g., going out for the occasional cup of coffee to relax with her friends). And as she made changes in her spending patterns, she began recognizing that the way she handled her money wasn't just external, but deeply personal and connected to her faith.

As recommended by the financial advisor, Sonya formed an accountability group with two other women who had been at the seminar. Together they developed plans for paying off debt and getting back on track. To avoid feeling overwhelmed, each woman chose just two things to work on at a time. Sonya felt like she was off to a great start.

But within a few weeks she got another call from her brother Raymond. He just needed a couple hundred dollars, he said, just to help get him back on his feet. Sonya waited for a few minutes before responding. Then she said, "How will this be any different than last time, Raymond? I'm beginning to see that the money I've been giving you isn't a good investment, and might even be part of the problem."

Raymond was stunned. He had expected the usual sympathy and help from his sister. "But I don't have a place to stay right now!" he protested. "And I need money to get back on my medication!" That night, he stayed at Sonya's place. And the next morning, she brought him to a community mental health center. A staff person there explained that their focus was on dealing with the underlying reasons Raymond kept going off his medication, and providing a support system to help him remain on it so he could hold down a job and support himself. Raymond felt betrayed by Sonya and was angry, but she left feeling that this was a place dedicated to longer-term solutions than her periodic bailouts could provide. She'd have to be okay with Raymond being angry at her.

Over the next six months, Sonya used a cash-only envelope system, kept track of all her spending, and met with her accountability group. She began giving again and was making payments on her loan. At times Sonya hit a few bumps in the road. When her car broke down unexpectedly, leaving her with a sizable repair bill, Sonya was angry and frustrated: "I'm being obedient here, God! Why now, when I'm trying so hard?"

Paying off her loan took three months longer than she had expected, but she did finally make the last payment. And on the day she did, she treated her accountability group to a dinner out. She knew where the money was coming from to do that, and instead of feeling compulsive, it felt generous. She felt free.

GROUP DISCUSSION QUESTIONS:

1. How would you describe your relationship with money?

2. What connections do you see between how you spend your money and what you value?

3. What do you feel God calling you to examine more deeply in the area of your finances?

4. What steps will you take to become a better manager of your money?

5. How is God prompting you to grow in generous giving?

SUGGESTED SCRIPTURE FOR MEMORIZATION:

Command those who are rich in this present world not to be arrogant nor to put their hope in wealth, which is so uncertain, but to put their hope in God, who richly provides us with everything for our enjoyment. Command them to do good, to be rich in good deeds, and to be generous and willing to share. In this way, they will lay up treasure for themselves as a firm foundation for the coming age, so that they may take hold of the life that is truly life. (1 Timothy 6:17-19)

CHAPTER 9

Toppling Idols

Isaac walked out of the restaurant after closing the deal and took a deep breath of fresh air. He had done it! This was a huge deal that had taken months of planning and he had finally closed it. Isaac felt elated. The sentence came into his mind fully formed: "This is the only place I feel alive." He recognized it imme-diately as true. How strange that he should feel alive in his work, but dead in so much else. Why was that?

When he got back to the office, he got pats on the back and congratulations all around. Isaac closed his door, sat down at his desk, and thought about it. He had always been a hard worker. He was good at the work he did and proud of it. He earned money for his family this way. Was there anything wrong with that? No, he told himself. But he didn't feel quite sure of that.

Why didn't he feel this sense of being alive around his wife, his kids, his friends? At work was where he felt confident and got a lot of recognition—it was only here that he felt a sense of worth.

■ ■ ■

Isaac is not alone in his discovery. We are all idolaters. Idolatry may sound like an extreme term, and may conjure up images of statues and strange rituals, but what does it really mean? Idolatry is simply putting something else in the place where God belongs—the place of worship, fulfillment, and worth.

We are all idolaters.

One of the most famous idols in the Bible was Baal—a god of stone the Hebrews discovered during their wilderness wanderings and were tempted to worship again and again throughout the following centuries. But today idols go way beyond Baal.

Idols can be anything: money, relationships, pleasure, security, addictions, etc. What robs us? What shifts our focus away from God? Whatever it is—that's an idol. They can look good from the outside—idols often do. But all idols shift our focus away from God, and all idols ultimately disappoint us. They fail to live up to their promises.

> **We need to identify the idols in our lives and then—strategically and intentionally—move them out of our lives. Within that vacant space, we can then invite God to dwell.**

How do we do that? Meditate on Colossians 3:1-17:

> Since, then, you have been raised with Christ, set your hearts on things above, where Christ is seated at the right hand of God. Set your minds on things above, not on earthly things. For you died, and your life is now hidden with Christ in God. When Christ, who is your life, appears, then you also will appear with him in glory.

> Put to death, therefore, whatever belongs to your earthly nature: sexual immorality, impurity, lust, evil desires and greed, which is idolatry. Because of these, the wrath of God is coming. You used to walk in these ways, in the life you once lived. But now you must also rid yourselves of all such things as these: anger, rage, malice, slander, and filthy language from your lips. Do not lie to each other, since you have taken off your old self with its practices and have put on the

new self, which is being renewed in knowledge in the image of its Creator. Here there is no Gentile or Jew, circumcised or uncircumcised, barbarian, Scythian, slave or free, but Christ is all, and is in all.

Therefore, as God's chosen people, holy and dearly loved, clothe yourselves with compassion, kindness, humility, gentleness and patience. Bear with each other and forgive one another if any of you has a grievance against someone. Forgive as the Lord forgave you. And over all these virtues put on love, which binds them all together in perfect unity.

Let the peace of Christ rule in your hearts, since as members of one body you were called to peace. And be thankful. Let the message of Christ dwell among you richly as you teach and admonish one another with all wisdom through psalms, hymns and songs from the Spirit, singing to God with gratitude in your hearts. And whatever you do, whether in word or deed, do it all in the name of the Lord Jesus, giving thanks to God the Father through him.

THE STARTING POINT

The starting point for all of this is being aware of our own tendencies. We all have different areas of struggle, no matter who we are. Moses lost his temper regularly. The apostle Paul had his unspecified "thorn in the flesh" (2 Corinthians 12:7-8). We all have our own besetting sins and problems, whether it's fear or pride or something else.

Look again at this sentence from the passage above (Colossians 3): "Put to death, therefore, whatever belongs to your earthly nature: sexual immorality, impurity, lust, evil desires and greed, which is idolatry." Compare the apostle Paul's list to the listing of the seven deadly sins:

✤ Lust   ✤ Gluttony   ✤ Greed
✤ Sloth (laziness) ✤ Wrath   ✤ Envy
✤ Pride

The list has had surprising staying power since it was first written by Pope Gregory the Great in the sixth century. The same sins still trail us today—only the window dressing has changed. And in a sense, each of the seven deadly sins is something good gone awry because we have begun worshipping it and using it in inappropriate ways. Sex, food, money/material possessions, relaxation, righteous anger over injustice, passion/desire, and legitimate pride in one's hard work or accomplishments—none of these things are wrong in and of themselves. In fact, they can all be good things when used well.

The same sins still trail us today—only the window dressing has changed.

Idols are about choices. When we choose something over God, it has become an idol. Jesus had a conversation with a young man in Matthew 19:16-23 about such choices:

> Just then a man came up to Jesus and asked, "Teacher, what good thing must I do to get eternal life?" "Why do you ask me about what is good?" Jesus replied. "There is only One who is good. If you want to enter life, keep the commandments." "Which ones?" he inquired. Jesus replied, "'You shall not murder, you shall not commit adultery, you shall not steal, you shall not give false testimony, honor your father and mother,' and 'love your neighbor as yourself.'" "All these I have kept," the young man said. "What do I still lack?" Jesus answered, "If you want to be perfect, go, sell your possessions and give to the poor, and you will have treasure in heaven. Then come, follow me." When the young man heard this, he went away sad, because he had great wealth. Then Jesus said to his disciples, "Truly I tell you, it is hard for the rich to enter the kingdom of heaven."

We can easily make an idol out of rules and get sidetracked on the dos and don'ts.

We all have something we are tempted to choose over God. For the rich young man in this story, that something was money—he struggled with greed. Those of us who look down on people with other struggles are more likely to be prone to pride—and tempted to choose church or our good reputations over God. We can easily make an idol out of rules and get sidetracked on the dos and don'ts. We are liable to do the same thing with the New Testament that the Pharisees did with the Old Testament: focusing on the individual rules without taking into account people or the underlying principles—the reasons the rules are there in the first place.

To uncover our own favored idols, we need to start asking ourselves some very difficult questions.

CHECKPOINTS:

- ❏ What do I think about most often?
- ❏ Where do I invest most of my time?
- ❏ Where do I invest most of my money?
- ❏ Where do I invest most of my energy?
- ❏ How does what I value line up with the scriptures?
- ❏ What would I be willing to give up and what would I have a hard time giving up?

Some idols are obvious: money, drugs, sex. Others are much more easily hidden: following the rules, pursuing excellence, recreation, the achievements of our children.

Anything—no matter how seemingly harmless—we choose over God becomes an idol. One pastor observed what he called "the worship of the soccer ball" in his church. The entire family life of many in his congregation revolved around soccer, even to the exclusion of spiritual formation in their kids.

Whatever our idols are, they create patterns of sin in our lives that ensnare us, trap us, and leave us unable to live out the good that God would have us do.

PROVERBS

- ✚ Proverbs: 5:22-23: The evil deeds of the wicked ensnare them; the cords of their sins hold them fast. For lack of discipline they will die, led astray by their own great folly.

- ✚ Proverbs 6:27-29: Can a man scoop fire into his lap without his clothes being burned? Can a man walk on hot coals without his feet being scorched? So is he who sleeps with another man's wife; no one who touches her will go unpunished.

THE GOLDEN CALF

As fallen people, we have a natural bent toward looking for idols. If we can't find one, we'll make one.

> ## *If we can't find an idol, we'll make one.*

When Moses went up the mountain for the ten commandments and seemed to be taking a little too long meeting with God, the Israelites back in the camp decided that they needed something a little more concrete to worship and they needed it right now. After all, they reasoned, who knew if Moses would even come back? So they pooled their jewelry and made a golden calf to worship. Somehow that golden calf felt safer to them than following an invisible, unpredictable God who seemed to be taking his time. (For the full story, see Exodus 32.)

Ultimately, the golden calf and the commandments of God could not coexist. The calf needed to be removed to make room for God. God does not share his place of worship. And it's no accident that the ten commandments begin with this:

> I am the LORD your God, who brought you out of Egypt, out of the land of slavery. You shall have no other gods before me. You shall not make for yourself an image in the form of anything in heaven above or on the earth beneath or in the waters below. You shall not bow down to them or worship them. (Exodus 20:2-5)

From there, the rest of the story of the Old Testament can be read as one long exercise in getting rid of idols.

TOPPLING IDOLS

Once we've identified our idols—and we all have some—what do we do about them? "Try harder to resist" is seldom a successful strategy. Any of us who have tried that route have tasted its futility. Instead, we need to recognize that this is a spiritual battle. We'll need to pray, invite the Holy Spirit to be at work in our lives, and then make some tough choices with that kind of power behind us. The choices we make will mean strategically removing these idols from our lives—and then filling that space with something else.

"Try harder to resist" is seldom a successful strategy.

Let's take a simple example: Say someone has decided that television has become an idol. She could try cutting back a bit, or resisting turning it on at certain times of the day. But she'd probably be more successful by making an intentional, clear-cut change. She could unplug it for a week. She could give the TV set away. And in the vacuum of time that is left, she'll need to find other activities to fill the void. Depending on her interests, she could spend more time outdoors, she could volunteer somewhere, she could read, she could spend more time with her friends, she could listen to music. And in some of that time previously spent watching TV, she could meet with God to worship him.

Let's look again at Colossians 3. We don't get rid of the bad only for the sake of getting rid of the bad. We fill the space with what is good. We take off the old self and put on the new self: "Do not lie to each other, since you have taken off your old self with its practices and have put on the new self, which is being renewed in knowledge in the image of its Creator" (Colossians 3:9-10).

In this way, what we are talking about in this chapter is not just self-help or improving our life. It is digging deeper into character formation and worship. In the place that formerly held idols, God is there.

CHECKPOINTS:
- ❏ Identify one idol in your life. Tell someone about it. Make a plan to topple it.
- ❏ Meditate on Colossians 3:1-17 this week. Read it aloud each day and reflect on it.
- ❏ Gather with a group of friends and discuss Ephesians 4:17-32 together.

FREED TO PURSUE GOD

Once there was a bush in my (Tara's) front yard that seemed stunted. It wasn't exactly dead, but it wouldn't grow either. My neighbor and I decided to move it to a location where it might get a bit more sun to see if that might revive it. As we dug and finally uprooted the bush, we discovered that the landscapers had not removed the original metal basket meant for transporting from around the roots of the bush. That grate served as an effective barrier to growth. No amount of water or sunshine or weeding made any difference as long as that metal basket was around the roots. Once the basket was removed, the bush began to grow.

That's what it's like when we get rid of idols. The barriers to our growth are removed. Now we can not only maintain, we can move ahead. We can begin thinking forward toward what God has for us to do. We can open ourselves up to his greater vision for our lives: "For we are God's handiwork, created in Christ Jesus to do good works, which God prepared in advance for us to do" (Ephesians 2:10).

freed from the cage of idolatry

Once we identify the idols in our lives—and strategically and intentionally move them out—we can then invite God to dwell with us in that space. We are freed from the cage of idolatry and can focus our energy on listening to God to see what he might have for us. And we are freed to pursue him with our whole heart.

■ ■ ■

Isaac walked away from the office that day with one question clear in his mind: Where's the line between being proud of my work and accomplishments and making an idol out of them? Isaac wasn't sure of the answer, but he did feel sure of the question. This was what he needed to be asking right now.

A couple days later Isaac met with the men from his early morning accountability group—Stephen, Ezra, and SaVaun. He told them how he'd been feeling and asked them what they thought. Ezra, who was older than the other men, said the only time he had felt like that—alive in one area, but dead in other more important areas—was at a time when he was getting himself into a lot of trouble. In his case it had been a woman other than his wife who brought about that feeling of being alive.

"I know what you're thinking," added Ezra, "that another woman is not the same thing at all. It's true that it's not the same thing, but it could just as easily have been something else moving my heart in another direction. Whenever you feel alive in one area and all the rest—family, friends, God—pales by comparison, that's when you know you're in trouble. That's a wake-up call."

Isaac walked away from that gathering feeling uncomfortable and a little angry. Was Ezra really saying this was as bad as all that? Isaac didn't think it was nearly as bad. Yet he couldn't shake Ezra's comment that it could have been something else that moved his heart in another direction. That did put a finger on the problem. That's exactly what this felt like—like his heart was moved in another direction, away from God.

So what should he do? He couldn't very well quit his job. That wasn't very realistic—and he'd just have to get another one anyway. How could he move his heart back in a different direction? He asked the friends in his group to pray for him, that he would know what to do.

Over the next couple months, Isaac made several choices at work that had a long-term impact. He turned down two new projects and referred them to newer employees. The newer employees were stunned, because these were good projects—the kind upper-level salespeople generally liked to hold onto for themselves. What an opportunity! Isaac also decided to leave the office at 5:00 pm every day, no matter what wasn't done. That was hard at first, but he had to remind himself that no one was going to live or die based on his leaving work on time. It would work out. And sure enough, he found that his hours at work were that much more productive.

With the extra time, Isaac had more time to relax with family and friends, and he felt more connected with God. It felt like a barrier had been removed. He no longer felt that sense of wanting to sneak off and get a little more work done.

Isaac also found a surprise benefit that he hadn't seen coming: he was really enjoying a mentoring-like relationship with the two new guys at work who had taken on his projects. They sought him out for advice and help. And Isaac felt better about investing in their development than he ever had about getting credit for his stellar sales records.

GROUP DISCUSSION QUESTIONS:

1. What are you hearing from God about idols?
2. To which of the seven deadly sins are you most prone?
3. What idols have you identified in your life?
4. What steps have you taken to remove idols from your life? How did that go?
5. How will you fill the space the idol leaves behind?

SUGGESTED SCRIPTURE FOR MEMORIZATION:

I am the LORD your God, who brought you out of Egypt, out of the land of slavery. You shall have no other gods before me. You shall not make for yourself an image in the form of anything in heaven above or on the earth beneath or in the waters below. You shall not bow down to them or worship them. (Exodus 20:2-5)

PART 3

Pouring Out: living as the hands and feet of Jesus

With the foundation of our relationship with God, self, and others established in part 1, and having discussed some practical ways we choose to live out those relationships in our day-to-day lives in part 2, we can now move fully into a life of love and service. We are freed to serve as the hands and feet of Jesus to the world around us.

From here, we can learn what it means for us to love others, embrace our gifts and calling, serve alongside others in the body of Christ, and make our own unique contribution to the kingdom of God.

Chapter 10: loving our neighbor
Whatever our plan looks like, we need to live with an outward focus—with the compassion of Jesus toward others. We need to live with an eye toward how we can bless others, reach out, engage, listen, and love.

Chapter 11: embracing our gifts and calling
God's intentions for us will align with our gifts, passions, and life context. We need to discern God's voice, discover who he has made us to be, and find ways to live out our giftedness and calling.

Chapter 12: teaming with others
To live out our calling, we need others alongside us. None of us is complete on our own. We all have a different part to play. Therefore, we need to learn how to work well with others toward a common goal.

Chapter 13: *making our kingdom contribution*

If we live well, as a disciple of Christ, following his guidance, we will leave a legacy. We will make a difference in this world and in the lives of others, patterning our lives along the last words of Jesus.

CHAPTER 10

Loving our neighbor as ourselves

Isaac felt like he'd grown so much over the last year. With the help of his men's group, he'd tackled staying centered when he was angry and he'd dealt with a workaholism that had been hard to own up to and even harder to deal with. And along the way he'd developed some close friends in his men's group that  met before work each Tuesday morning: SaVaun, Stephen, and Ezra. They prayed together, read scripture together, challenged each other, and shared life together. And Stephen had come to know Jesus as they met.

Isaac was content, but he still sensed something was missing. It seemed like there was something more out there. He longed to reach out beyond himself, to make a difference in the world, in people's lives. But how?

> We are all called to reach out—to make a difference in the lives of those around us. All of us are to live with an outward focus, expressing the compassion of Jesus toward others. We need to live with an eye toward how we can bless others, reach out, engage, listen, and love. In doing so, we develop authentic, redemptive relationships with those around us.

Jesus was once asked a great question—essentially, "What's most important?"

> One of them, an expert in the law, tested him with this question: "Teacher, which is the greatest commandment in the Law?" Jesus replied: "'Love the Lord your God with all your heart and with all your soul and with all your mind.' This is the first and greatest commandment. And the second is like it: 'Love your neighbor as yourself.' All the Law and the Prophets hang on these two commandments." (Matthew 22:35-40)

This is the life we were designed to be living: Loving God and loving others. Loving others flows out of our life with God: We love because he first loved us (1 John 4:19).

But in real life, what does it look like to love others? If we are going to live it out, it needs to be more than a fuzzy feeling or a nice idea. How do we put hands and feet to the idea of loving others? Alan Hirsch suggests that if we eat with three people a week, bless three people a week, and spend one hour a week with God, we'll be living as Jesus intended. That seems like a good rule of thumb; let's fill that out a bit. What can loving others look like?

- ✤ It looks like the teenager willing to risk social alienation by standing up to his friends on behalf of an uncool kid they're pushing around.
- ✤ It looks like the teacher who lets go of assuming her way is the right way, the only way, and risks considering new views, approaching kids in her class differently and with more compassion.
- ✤ It looks like the pastor who is willing to share his failings and shortcomings even though he fears it will undercut his spiritual authority.

✤ It looks like the couple who invites their homosexual neighbors over for dinner and treats them just as they would any other couple.

✤ It looks like the young man who volunteers to tutor at an inner-city school, staying even when the kids act like they don't want him around—because he knows so many others haven't stayed in their lives.

✤ It looks like the woman who co-facilitates an anger management group for women at the Salvation Army and brings them homemade crepes, knowing these women haven't had anything homemade for them in a long time.

✤ It looks like the doctor who spends his Saturday mornings providing health care for the uninsured.

✤ It looks like the parent at the bus stop who sees another parent crying and stops to ask what's wrong.

✤ It looks like the man who engages his friend in spiritual conversation and then does more listening than talking.

The possibilities are limitless—and so are the people to love.

WHO IS MY NEIGHBOR?

When Jesus answered the question, "What must I do to inherit eternal life?" the man who asked it had an important follow-up question:

> But he wanted to justify himself, so he asked Jesus, "And who is my neighbor?"
>
> In reply Jesus said: "A man was going down from Jerusalem to Jericho, when he fell into the hands of robbers. They stripped him of his clothes, beat him and went away, leaving him half dead. A priest happened to be going down the same road, and when he saw the man, he passed by on the other side. So too, a Levite, when he came to the place and saw him, passed by on the other side. But a Samaritan, as he traveled, came where the man was; and when he saw him, he took pity on him. He went to him and bandaged his wounds, pouring on oil and wine. Then he put the man on his own donkey, brought him to an inn and took care of him. The next day he took out two denarii and gave them to the innkeeper. 'Look after him,' he said, 'and when I return, I will reimburse you

for any extra expense you may have.' Which of these three do you think was a neighbor to the man who fell into the hands of robbers?" The expert in the law replied, "The one who had mercy on him." Jesus told him, "Go and do likewise." (Luke 10:29-37)

Jesus calls us to show his love to *all* people:

To find our neighbor, Jesus simply asks us to look around us. Anyone we run across—however accidentally—is our neighbor. That includes everyone—whether they are like us or not, the kind and the unkind, the righteous and the sinner, the Christian and the non-Christian. Jesus calls us to show his love to all people:

You have heard that it was said, "Love your neighbor and hate your enemy." But I tell you: Love your enemies and pray for those who persecute you, that you may be children of your Father in heaven. He causes his sun to rise on the evil and the good, and sends rain on the righteous and the unrighteous. If you love those who love you, what reward will you get? Are not even the tax collectors doing that? And if you greet only your own people, what are you doing more than others? Do not even pagans do that? (Matthew 5:43-47)

PROVERBS:

- ✤ Proverbs 22:2: Rich and poor have this in common: The LORD is the Maker of them all.
- ✤ Proverbs 29:13: The poor and the oppressor have this in common: The LORD gives sight to the eyes of both.

WHERE DO WE START?

When we look around us in that way, we can see all sorts of needs. Sometimes too many, leaving us feeling overwhelmed. With so many possible good things to do, where do we even start? The number of choices can leave us feeling paralyzed. Which needs do we meet?

The key is to figure out where we connect best. Start with two questions: What do I like to do? How can I serve/contribute? We see the needs, then we match up our skills and desires in a practical way by looking around us and identifying the connections we already have. It doesn't have to be some huge shift—we can each start wherever we are. One woman was regularly visiting a relative in a hospice and decided to broaden her involvement there to include some of the other residents. After all, she was well-suited to this type of ministry, bringing a calm spirit and a listening ear to the bedsides—and those aren't abilities to be taken for granted.

Figuring out where we connect best can start simply. I (Tara) like to read. How can that translate into loving others? Some connections I've found in the past have resulted in my joining a book club and getting to know the other people there, reading to the kindergarten class at my kids' school, and taking one-on-one time with second-graders who need some extra practice reading to an adult. Whatever our areas of interest include, whatever our abilities and experiences are, we can use them to love and serve others. That can—and does—look a million different ways.

Most of the time we don't recognize all the opportunities around us. A prayer walk in our neighborhood can open our eyes. Maybe we could help our neighbor install that screen door they've been working on. Maybe we can shovel the snow off our elderly neighbors' sidewalk. Maybe we could connect with another family with toddlers down the street. The more ways we can live, serve, and play alongside those around us, the better.

One young man has always enjoyed playing basketball. He took a prayer walk around his own neighborhood and saw an inner-city school where he could volunteer as an assistant basketball coach. It's one of the poorest high schools in the city, but the coach has a vision for helping the boys on the team become better men. They need role models, people who care, people who will make—and keep—their commitments. This man is making a difference by loving his neighbors.

CHECKPOINT:

✤ A woman likes to cook. How many different ways can you come up with that she might be able to use that area of interest to love and serve others?

CHECKPOINT:

❖ What kind of life do you want to live? Discuss the seven questions below with a coach, a disciple, or a close friend.

The first three are geared toward loving God:

1. How are you deepening your experience of God?
2. How is God changing your life?
3. How has the Holy Spirit been prompting you?

And the next four are geared toward loving others:

4. In what ways are you being genuine with those around you?
5. How have you had opportunity to value people?
6. How are you relationally engaged with others?
7. How have you been the hands and feet of Jesus?

INTENTIONALLY SPONTANEOUS

Asking each other questions like the ones above move us toward living the kind of life we want to live. They help us explore our options and become aware of the possibilities. They help us become more intentional about how we can love and serve others. And paradoxically, being intentional allows us to be more spontaneous and open to the leading of the Spirit.

A man had been praying throughout the week that God would show him practical ways to love others. He asked that God would prepare him to be open to the promptings of the Spirit and to be open to the unexpected. This man was out one day and had to pick up something for lunch. He'd been trying to eat more healthily, but a particular fast food restaurant kept coming to mind. He just couldn't seem to think of any other places nearby. So he went there, and he met a man who had lost his job and had his money stolen. He was able to meet a need by buying this man a meal and getting him connected to a local food bank.

In another case of intentional spontaneity, a thirteen-year-old girl found herself continuing to think about homeless people. She was facing a lot of challenges herself, but she had a heart for the homeless and truly cared about them. So she and her foster mom prepared small care packages to keep in the car—bags with toothpaste, protein bars, and other non-perishable foods and toiletries. She decorated the bags and gave them out whenever she saw people in need. She was prepared to be spontaneously giving. This girl was able to make a difference even at a time of life when she had a lot of needs herself.

That's how we can live a life open to the promptings of the Holy Spirit and prepared to respond: Follow your heart, be open to the Spirit, and meet the needs of others. That's what Jesus modeled for us. He listened to Father and paid attention to those around him. He went to where the needs were—the sick, the dying, the hungry, the prostitutes, the lepers, the ones no one else would touch.

I (Bob) was recently riding in a taxi in Chicago with my ministry partner, Jon. The cab driver was using some pretty colorful language. Then he asked us, "So what do you do?" "We start churches." The cab driver was immediately apologetic about his language. Jon said, "No, it's okay. We're not offended." "So," asked the cab driver, trying to get back on track, "What denomination are you with?" "We're just trying to follow Jesus and go back to the basics—meeting people wherever they are," explained Jon. "In fact," I interjected, "you could help us here. If Jesus were in Chicago, what would he be doing?" The taxi driver thought about it and responded, "Well, I guess he'd be hanging out with sinners. Come to think of it, we're all sinners, so he'd probably be hanging out with the sinner-sinners."

Unchurched people know what authentic living would look like. They know what Jesus would be doing and where he'd be going. And he wouldn't be hanging out in the churches. He'd be loving sinners. Unchurched people want to see us follow in his footsteps. They want to see us be the hands and feet of Jesus: neighbors that will care, people who will hang out with the disenfranchised, the hurting.

COMBATING BUSYNESS AND PRIORITIZING RELATIONSHIPS

Loving our neighbor, hanging out with sinners, advocating for the helpless. Sounds great, but where would we find the time? After all, we have jobs, we have lives, we have dinners to cook and dishes to wash and bills to pay.

Living as Jesus did likely means we'll need to make some changes in our lives. We'll need to combat busyness and we'll need to prioritize relationships. That can be countercultural and difficult to do, but it is the way Jesus has called us to live. Jesus, with all that he had to do, was never too busy to love and serve those around him.

Ideally, we can connect with others and serve them in the course of our daily lives anyway. It's not usually a matter of taking time out to serve, but incorporating service wherever we already are. Of course, if our lives are insulated in such a way that we don't serve, we may need to listen to the prompting of the Holy Spirit and adjust our schedules accordingly.

As we connect with God, and as he is changing us, then we reach out to others in love and service. Each of us needs to figure out how God wants us to contribute to living missionally and building redemptive relationships. It'll look a bit different for each of us, but the basic principle is quite simple. As a very wise man once said, "Success is finding out what God wants you to do and doing it."

Whatever that plan looks like for us, we need to find a way to live with an outward focus so we can express the compassion of Jesus toward others. As we bless others through serving, listening, reaching out, and loving them, we'll build the kind of redemptive relationships that Jesus called us to.

By mixing with people we may not normally associate with, God can grow us all. Sometimes different types of people can influence each other in positive ways. In this sense, we are good for those who don't know Christ, and they are good for us. Together we are both stronger.

■ ■ ■

Isaac prayed with his men's group and with his wife, Tasha, about how he could best make a difference. How did God want to use him? He spent about a month seeking God on that question. One day he was talking with Tasha about it when she said, "Well, what has God made you good at?" The simplicity  of her question stopped him in his tracks. He'd had such a hard time deciding on a profession, because what he really enjoyed was being with people and talking with people. And generally you don't get paid just to hang out. The closest fit he'd found was his sales job. He had a lot of interaction with people in his current role and he enjoyed it.

But now, as he felt called to invest in others more deeply, it suddenly all made sense. God had always used him in the context of his personal relationships. That's how God had designed him. And when he looked around him, he could see all the gaps where deeper community and connection was needed, where networks of relationships could be formed.

So Isaac decided to be strategic about his relationships—something he'd never thought of doing before. Stephen, from his men's group, had just recently come to know Christ, and Isaac went out of his way to meet Stephen's friends and hang out with them. He served them, befriended them, and engaged in spiritual conversation with them. Some were receptive to the gospel and some were not, but that made no difference in the respect Isaac showed them. Soon Stephen and some of his friends formed their own men's group to pray, read scripture together, and support one another.

Isaac also began investing more in the two new guys he was mentoring at work. They were just starting out in sales and were also new in town and didn't know a lot of people yet. He and Tasha invited them and their wives over for dinner. It was a little chaotic with the twins, but everyone had a great time. Isaac began praying about how he could share the love of Jesus with these couples he and Tasha were beginning to get to know.

Isaac had come a long way. He could feel the Spirit pouring from his life into the lives of those around him. And he was grateful to experience God working through him to create redemptive, transformative relationships.

GROUP DISCUSSION QUESTIONS:

1. Who do you know in your circle of influence that you can serve?

2. What groups of people are you hesitant to reach out to? What does that tell you?

3. When you look around, what opportunities do you see to serve others?

4. Who is God calling you to invest in relationally?

5. How do you sense God wanting to use you?

SUGGESTED SCRIPTURE FOR MEMORIZATION:

If you love those who love you, what reward will you get? Are not even the tax collectors doing that? And if you greet only your own people, what are you doing more than others? Do not even pagans do that? (Matthew 5:46-47)

CHAPTER 11

Embracing our gifts and calling

Harry had been off drugs for two years now, and involved in his church for a year and a half. His life had seen a lot of changes. He had reconciled with his son and done what he could to make peace with his wife and daughter. He was a regular at his support and recovery group and had taken on some of the  facilitation responsibility. He had some good friends there. He'd done a lot of inner work and had come a long way in learning to control his temper and take responsibility for his own life and choices. He'd gotten a job as a mechanic, which he enjoyed: "Cars are a lot easier to fix than people," he'd tell customers who came into the shop. Harry felt grounded—something he hadn't felt in a really long time.

He was working on his eleventh step: "Sought through prayer and meditation to improve our conscious contact with God *as we understood him*, praying only for knowledge of his will for us and the power to carry that out."

On the advice of the support group leader, Harry had been taking silent retreats to reflect and to hear God's voice. He didn't have enough money to get out of town or go to any fancy retreat centers, so he'd just spend a morning in the park a couple times a month. He'd find a secluded, shady spot and pray. Sometimes he'd journal; sometimes he'd sit in silence.

Harry thought about the eleventh step: conscious contact with God, praying for knowledge of God's will. What did God want from him? What should he do? Harry remembered the question that had come to him when he'd first thought about visiting the church: "What, if anything, do I have to offer? With my history and so much wasted time already, what could God really use me for?" He knew by now that God did want to use him, but the jury was still out on what God might want to use him for.

■ ■ ■

God desires to use us to further his purposes: "For I know the plans I have for you," declares the LORD, "plans to prosper you and not to harm you, plans to give you hope and a future" (Jeremiah 29:11).

We need to discern God's voice, discover who he has made us to be, then find ways to live out our giftedness and calling. We all need to ask the questions Harry is asking, "What is God's will for me? What does God want to use me for?" God's intentions for us will align with both our passions—what we care about—and our context—the real situations of our life and experience. Then, as we step into his will and begin living it out, we'll bring that vision into sharper focus.

Discerning God's Voice

We all hear God's voice in different ways. Review and practice some of the strategies from chapter two on connecting with God. Try a variety of ways to hear his voice, remembering that different approaches work for different people at different stages of life. We too often limit ourselves unnecessarily.

Also, we need to remember that God doesn't always answer our direct questions. Sometimes what he most wants to tell us isn't the answer to what we're asking. And sometimes we're asking the wrong questions all together. In discerning God's will, usually open-ended questions like "What would you like me to do?" yield more response than, "Should I do such-and-such or not?"

A man named Brad once worked with a college-and-career group. The group was filled with twenty-somethings wanting to know what God's will for them was. What job should they do? Who should they date or marry? They had prayed but weren't getting clear answers. Some of them were delaying doing anything at all for years while they waited for God to respond.

Brad gave them this career advice: "Pick something you enjoy—and that isn't immoral—and do it!" His relationship advice was similar: "Choose a godly woman (or man) you're attracted to and ask her out."

God's will wasn't hidden cleverly like a needle in a haystack

And somehow that "there's-no-one-right-answer" approach was freeing. God's will wasn't hidden cleverly like a needle in a haystack that God wanted to make especially difficult to find. And in the very act of moving forward, the learning began and God's will unfolded more clearly.

It's like that with our ministry calling as well. How can we bless others? There are so many possible ways that would be good and helpful. And sometimes God is not clear about which way we should go. So, after trying to discern his will, we need to step forward and try something. And in the process will come the learning. Through this back-and-forth, give-and-take process of listening to God and moving forward, we begin to understand more about how God has designed us and how he can use us. Taking this type of process approach frees us from the fear of having to get everything exactly right: we can make adjustments as we go.

PROVERBS:

+ Proverbs 14:22: Do not those who plot evil go astray? But those who plan what is good find love and faithfulness.
+ Proverbs 16:9: In their hearts human beings plan their course, but the LORD establishes their steps.

✜ Proverbs 20:24: A person's steps are directed by the LORD. How then can anyone understand their own way?

DISCOVERING YOUR GIFTS

In addition to hearing God's voice, we also need to discover how he has made us. What are our spiritual gifts? What are we good at? What are we passionate about? What do we have to contribute? All of these questions will play a role in helping us develop a vision for our lives and ministry.

We can begin by discovering our spiritual gifts. Each believer has at least one spiritual gift, placed in us by the Holy Spirit when we first received him. There are many different listings of spiritual gifts. No one knows for sure how many there are, but here are some of those listed in scripture:

Romans 12:	1 Corinthians 12 adds:	Ephesians 4 adds:
prophecy	wisdom	evangelist
serving	knowledge	pastor
teaching	faith	
encouraging	healing	
giving	miraculous powers	
leading	distinguishing between spirits	
mercy	speaking in tongues	
	interpreting tongues	
	apostles	
	helping	
	guidance	

Take note that many of the spiritual gifts have corresponding commands for all believers. For example, although some might have the spiritual gift of giving, God expects all of us to give. So if we are obedient, then we can try a lot of different things and see what God blesses. That approach would help us discover our giftedness.

Each of us has been given one of these gifts to use for the advance of the kingdom of God. So how do we know which gifts we have? When we use a gift it's effective, it's fulfilling, and it's energizing. Although there are many spiritual gifts tests, probably the best way to discover our gifts is to try to use them, see how it feels, then allow our community to provide feedback. Spiritual gifts are best confirmed by others. They can often see our gifts more clearly than we can ourselves.

Shortly after becoming a Christian as a teenager, I (Tara) tried the trial-and-error method of finding my spiritual gifts. I looked over a listing of spiritual gifts and decided to try some out and see if they fit. However, sometimes the gifts we want are not the ones we have. I tried helping with the worship at the youth group I was attending. Since this involved actual singing, it didn't go very well. I also tried teaching children, but that just left me frustrated and exhausted. For a while, I wanted to be a counselor, but discovered that I apparently lacked the gift of mercy as well. This was turning out to be harder than I'd expected.

Spiritual gifts are best confirmed by others.

Some of my friends at youth group gave me suggestions based on what they saw. A possible gift mentioned by more than one was administration. I felt almost like someone had just insulted me. Administration? That was a pretty boring gift. Not very spiritual either—wasn't it just being organized? And yet God has used it in many ways over time, combined with other gifts and interests, helping me understand its value in context.

GROUP EXERCISE FOR DISCOVERING SPIRITUAL GIFTS:

Participate as a group in various service and outreach activities over a period of months. Try to engage in a wide variety of ways. Then discuss the following questions in your group:

- ✦ What activity most energized you?
- ✦ Where do you feel you were most effective?
- ✦ When do you most feel like you're making a difference?
- ✦ What most stirs your heart?
- ✦ What gets you righteously angry?
- ✦ If time and resources weren't an issue, where would you make a difference?

As we think through questions like these, we'll need to be sure to invite feedback from others regarding what they've observed in us.

Once we've discovered our gifts, we'll need to commit to using them for the benefit of others. God did not give them to us to hoard but to share. Their purpose is the building up of the body as we move forward toward the kingdom of God.

CHECKPOINTS:

Possible ways to try using our spiritual gifts

❏ Teaching: teach a class at church, teach children's church, tutor in a volunteer program.

❏ Hospitality: host a small group, throw parties for your neighbors, invite people over for dinner

❏ Intercession: pray for the kingdom of God, pray for other leaders and intercessors, talk with others about prayer

❏ Mercy: visit the sick and the dying, volunteer in a hospice, listen to others

❏ Administration: streamline the effectiveness of a ministry, organize a neighborhood outreach, plan a mission trip

EXERCISE:

Connecting our passions with our spiritual gifts

✤ Write down a few of the things you would most like to change in the world (e.g. homelessness, loneliness, the spread of the gospel message). Now consider your own gifts and see where you could find connections. For example, say one of the things you care most about is evangelism, but you don't have the gift of evangelism or preaching. Say your gifts are hospitality and mercy. How could you use these gifts toward evangelistic ends? One option might be hosting a dinner gathering for neighbors. How many other connections can you find?

GIFTEDNESS INFORMS CALLING

Our giftedness informs our calling. Calling, simply defined, is what God wants us to do. It doesn't have to be complicated, and it doesn't have to be exact. Use a learn-as-you-go approach. But God doesn't give his spiritual gifts to us randomly; he gives them to us for a reason. He wants us to use them to further his kingdom. Our calling is what God wants us to do.

In some ways, we could say that God wants the same thing from all of us. Jesus called all of his disciples to love God, love others, and make disciples. He has called all of us to be generous, to serve others, and to live out the fruit of the Spirit: love, joy, peace, patience, kindness, goodness, faithfulness, gentleness, and self-control (Galatians 5:22-23).

And yet the Holy Spirit has given each of us specific spiritual gifts that he wants us to use. One man who came to faith as an adult felt that he was not particularly generous. He could see from the scriptures that God called everyone to give financially, but he knew that this would be particularly difficult for him. It just didn't come naturally. He told God, "If you want me to give, you're going to have to make me feel the needs. When I cry, I'll give."

Turns out that although giving wasn't a natural gift for him, it was a supernatural one. God took this man up on his offer, and he suddenly found himself crying over the needs around him. The Holy Spirit had given him the spiritual gift of giving. He has exercised it well over the years, and his heart has been continually softened in the process.

Our calling will be informed by how God has gifted us. Chances are that some of the things you thought of doing in previous chapters are aligned with your spiritual gifts.

FINDING OUT WHAT GOD WANTS YOU TO DO

God requires our active participation in living out our calling: "Take delight in the LORD and he will give you the desires of your heart. Commit your way to the LORD; trust in him and he will do this" (Psalm 37:4-5). As we grow closer to God, our heart becomes more like God's heart, so the desires we have and the requests we make are more in line with what he desires.

In the context of this relationship with God, we need to have an open heart and a listening ear. Here are some categories that may help bring your calling to light:

UNEARTHING YOUR PASSIONS: What do you care about? What do you value? What do you think is important? There are many different ministries that are part of the kingdom of God and they're all important. But which ones do you personally care most about? Children? Poverty in the inner city? People using their spiritual gifts? Helping people understand and live out God's word? Although as followers of

Jesus, we should all care about what he cares about and engage in a number of different areas, not everything can be done by every person. We are of most use to the kingdom if we focus our energy on areas where God has given us passion. One woman created an entire small business geared toward helping women who wanted to get out of the sex trade to secure other employment.

LOOKING AT YOUR OWN HISTORY AND EXPERIENCE: In many cases, our vision is born out of our own pain. Think of the recovering addicts who come to schools to talk with kids about drugs. Think of the sick child who grows up to become a doctor or medical researcher. Often our past experience points us in the direction of our future vision—how we are called to invest the rest of our lives. My (Bob's) experience of the pain of being a new church planter without having the resources I needed led me down the path of coaching church planters and creating resources for them. The roots of who we become are more often than not found in our stories.

ASSESSING THE SOIL: Before we can fully clarify our vision, we need to understand the opportunities and limitations of our lives. We all have different contexts that others don't have. How can we make the best use of where we are in life? Ministry is never done in isolation, but in the full context of our lives. That includes our families, where we live, experiences we bring to the table, what we understand and what we don't. A man who is heavily involved in a successful racial reconciliation ministry shares that he would never have been able to do this ministry had it not been for some very negative experiences he'd had growing up as a black male in America. God uses the greater context of our lives: "You intended to harm me, but God intended it for good to accomplish what is now being done, the saving of many lives" (Genesis 50:20).

Thinking through these three categories, as well as your spiritual gifts, can help bring God's desires for you into clearer focus.

EXERCISES:

✦ Although it can be hard to identify strengths and gifts in ourselves, it's often much easier with others. Tell three people this week something that you admire about them—a strength or a gift that they have.

✦ Find a scripture passage that best represents your vision for your contribution to the kingdom.

LIVING OUT YOUR CALLING

God has great things in store for us. "For we are God's handiwork, created in Christ Jesus to do good works, which God prepared in advance for us to do" (Ephesians 2:10). We can accomplish a great deal for the kingdom, but we don't need to do it alone. Keep on going to the next chapter—God has other handiwork too. We all need help staying on track as we move forward toward all that God has for us.

> *Very few things in life that are worth doing are easy.*

Even though we may not see all of our calling, we can take the next steps. Very few things in life that are worth doing are easy. But when we start by asking, "What does God want to use me for?" and then move forward using our gifts in faith, we embrace the calling God has on our lives. And we can accomplish amazing things for the kingdom.

■ ■ ■

Harry engaged in a few months of reflection, trying to discern God's voice. Whenever he thought he heard it, he'd try journaling about the ideas that came to him, playing with them and trying them on. Eventually, he hit upon one idea that seemed to stick. It used his skills and experience, it served others, and Harry  received confirmation from some close friends that this seemed to be from God.

A few months later, after a good deal of planning and organizing, Harry started a job placement ministry for people in recovery. He met with people in free public places, listening to them and reflecting back their strengths, trying to help them deal with the obstacles that blocked their path to secure employment. Sometimes he showed patience and compassion. Other times he confronted counterproductive behaviors. It just depended on what he sensed that the person needed.

He met with some success. Several people found jobs that worked out. Harry signed up for some coach training offered through his church so that he could learn to become a better listener and ask better questions as he helped people explore their options. His enjoyment of this ministry increased along with his increasing skills. And he began to see God using his own experiences—both the positive and the negative—to help others.

Over time, Harry realized this ministry was bridging him from his eleventh step into his twelfth: "Having had a spiritual awakening as the result of these steps, we tried to carry this message to others, and to practice these principles in all our affairs." And a passage came to mind, which he decided to commit to memory: "And the things you have heard me say in the presence of many witnesses entrust to reliable people who will also be qualified to teach others" (2 Timothy 2:2). For Harry, this was what passing it on looked like.

GROUP DISCUSSION QUESTIONS:

1. After reading this chapter, what struck you most as a potential next step God may be asking of you?

2. What are some beliefs you've held about God's will or his plan for you?

3. What are three gifts or strengths that you have?

4. What are some of your deepest passions? Things you care most about?

5. What are some of your life experiences—either positive or negative—that could be used to help others?

6. What resources will you need to help your vision become a reality?

SUGGESTED SCRIPTURE FOR MEMORIZATION:

"For I know the plans I have for you," declares the LORD, "plans to prosper you and not to harm you, plans to give you hope and a future." (Jeremiah 29:11)

CHAPTER 12

Teaming with others

The midweek kids' club was really taking off. All kinds of new kids had been flowing into the gatherings, many of them from families that didn't attend church. Maria was excited by the possibilities. This season would bring so many great opportunities. Her head was spinning with all kinds of ideas. If they could involve more teen helpers, they could continue to expand the ministry and really reach this neighborhood.

The only problem really lay with Scott, as far as Maria was concerned. Scott was the other adult volunteer for the midweek kids' club—her ministry partner. He was great with the kids, very caring and patient, but as far as Maria could tell he just seemed to lack any kind of vision for what the future could hold. He seemed happy with the status quo and even mentioned not bringing in more kids because the program was full and he didn't want the quality to be affected. How shortsighted! Maria felt herself getting frustrated even thinking about it.

She had found it difficult to work with Scott in the past because he was always focusing on the details instead of the big picture. Whenever she had a great idea, he'd deflate the balloon by asking how they would actually pull that off or by bringing up objections about why it won't work. Although Maria had found that kind of behavior annoying in the past, the stakes were even higher now. She just couldn't see letting this opportunity go. Maybe she could talk to the pastor. If he understood the situation, surely he'd find a suitable replacement for Scott.

■ ■ ■

Sometimes teaming with others is not much fun. Getting along with people can be difficult, especially when we think we're supposed to be working toward a common goal. We've all had times when we've gotten frustrated with those who are serving alongside us. And there are a lot of different ways we can handle that frustration. But the first step is acknowledging that we need one another.

> ## *We need each other—even the people who annoy us.*

> **If we are to engage in effective ministry and live out our calling, we need each other. We even need the people who annoy us. In fact, sometimes the very differences that annoy us are exactly the areas where we can most benefit one another. We are different because we all have a different part to play.**

God seems to have designed it this way. Numerous times the apostle Paul compares the church to a human body (Romans 12, I Corinthians 12, Ephesians 4, Colossians 1). We need all the parts for it to function the way it's supposed to. Each of us plays an essential role in the body of Christ. None of us can do it all alone; we need the other parts. Instead of trying to be everything, we need to learn to lean on each other. We need to learn to appreciate each other and work well with others who are different from us. If we are the hands, can we appreciate the feet? If we are the ears, can we appreciate the eyes? We need to see the value in each other, as the body would be incomplete without any one of its parts. And together, we can accomplish far greater things than either of us could do alone.

> ## *Together we can accomplish far greater things.*

Easier said than done though, isn't it? Sometimes other parts of the body seem like they're actively trying to thwart what we're doing. If we are the eyes, we may be focused on where we're trying to go. But the ears hear something potentially dangerous that brings the whole body to a complete stop. Yes, our path has been thwarted, at least temporarily, but for a good reason. We need to look around to see what it was that the ears heard. Each of us needs each other to get the overall job done well. An African proverb says, "If you want to run fast, run alone. If you want to run far, run together."

FILLING IN THE GAPS

We can work side by side, each using our own gifts, but we also need each other to help fill in our own gaps. Once we know who we are, then we'll need to ask who we need. Who can be strong where we are weak?

Just as we all have strengths, we also all have weaknesses, limitations, and blind spots. And just as others can often identify our strengths with more accuracy, others can also help us identify our limiting factors. Those are the areas where we'll need others to help fill in their strengths where we are weak.

If we are great on vision, but short on organization—we'll need help. If we are great at making others feel comfortable, but short on challenging them toward growth—we'll need help. If we push through toward the goal, but lose sight of the relationships—we'll need help.

> *To accomplish our calling—we'll need help. Many of our strengths have corresponding weaknesses.*

Many of our strengths have corresponding weaknesses. We need to know our own weaknesses and then surround ourselves with others who can help us in those areas. Working together with others helps us make the most of our strengths while making our weaknesses less of a problem. We need others around us. I (Bob) have often told people, "If you want to know my weaknesses, identify the strengths of the people around me."

APPRECIATING THOSE WHO ARE DIFFERENT THAN YOU

Often we have strengths in a certain area because we value that area. Let's take the example of someone who is focused on getting things done. That person may believe that getting things done is important—which it is. He may focus on goals and moving toward those goals, and as a result he may be very strong in those areas. However, he may also tend to forget about the relationships along the way—something that is also important.

Often what happens in that scenario is someone who is focused on results begins to think in either/or terms instead of both/and terms: we must choose either results or relationships. This way of thinking results in competition rather than cooperation—we must say relationships are unimportant in order to say results are important.

If we are results-oriented, we begin viewing those who are attending to the relationships as slackers, not working toward accomplishing the vision. We view them as expending sideways energy rather than forward energy. We get irritated with them because they do things differently than we would. And working well with them becomes increasingly difficult.

> *We get irritated with those who do things differently than we would.*

These tensions are not new. The apostle Paul dealt with them in the first-century church, and here's the advice he had for them:

Just as a body, though one, has many parts, but all its many parts form one body, so it is with Christ. For we were all baptized by one Spirit so as to form one body—whether Jews or Gentiles, slave or free—and we were all given the one Spirit to drink. Even so the body is not made up of one part but of many.

Now if the foot should say, "Because I am not a hand, I do not belong to the body," it would not for that reason cease to be part of the body. And if the ear should say, "Because I am not an eye, I do not belong to the body," it would not for that reason cease to be part of the body. If the whole body were an eye, where would the sense of hearing be? If the whole body were an ear, where would the sense of smell be? But in fact God has placed the parts in the body, every one of them, just as he wanted them to be. If they were all one part, where would the body be? As it is, there are many parts, but one body.

The eye cannot say to the hand, "I don't need you!" And the head cannot say to the feet, "I don't need you!" On the contrary, those parts of the body that seem to be weaker are indispensable, and the parts that we think are less honorable we treat with special honor. And the parts that are unpresentable are treated with special modesty, while our presentable parts need no special treatment. But God has put the body together, giving greater honor to the parts that lacked it, so that there should be no division in the body, but that its parts should have equal concern for each other. If one part suffers, every part suffers with it; if one part is honored, every part rejoices with it. (1 Corinthians 12:12-26)

No matter what our role, we all belong to the body. Each of us is necessary and important. And we are all connected. Only together can we accomplish the vision God has set before us. We need to seek out people who are strong where we are weak—and respect them enough to allow them the freedom to work where they are gifted and strong.

WHO DO YOU NEED?

In the last chapter we talked about giftedness and calling. Maybe there's something God has been putting on our heart, but we're not the one to lead it. We can begin to pray and ask God what he wants us to do. We can ask him to show us our part. After all, any movement of God is birthed in prayer. We can also begin to talk with others. Maybe God is speaking to them as well. If one person has the gift of mercy and one has the gift of serving, together they'll be stronger—and go further—than either would have alone.

One man had a passion for reading the Bible and encouraging others to read along with him. A friend of his was tech-savvy and a networker. Together they started a blog that encourages people to read through the Bible in one year alongside them. They provide encouragement and thoughts along the way. When we team with others whose gifts complement ours, we can look to see where God is at work and cooperate with him. Not all of us are called to be the point person for a ministry, but we can all ask God what he wants us to do—and who else we need to help see that vision become a reality.

In my work starting a network of missional house churches, I (Bob) have found that teaming with others is absolutely essential. No matter who has the original idea for a service project or outreach, that person needs to have someone else along with them.

> Also, if two lie down together, they will keep warm.
>> But how can one keep warm alone?
> Though one may be overpowered,
>> two can defend themselves.
>> A cord of three strands is not quickly broken.
> (Ecclesiastes 4:11-12)

Sometimes the best ideas are those that are thought up by people who have a heart for some particular kind of ministry, but they themselves aren't the leader. They need a blend of others who are different from them to make a good team. And together, they can create a more sustainable ministry. We need to have the support of others to keep moving forward over the long haul—people to pray with and people to talk with to discern where God may be leading next.

DEVELOPING A COMMON VISION: SOME TEAM ACTIVITIES

A vision may initially come to one person, but for a group of believers to bring that vision to reality, it must be shared. All must be invited to contribute ideas toward that vision as God fills out the picture of what it could look like. Often he gives only a sliver of vision at first that becomes more and more fully expressed as the body of Christ develops it together. We may have ideas based on our passions and gifts and what we've heard from God. Yet when we are working with a team, others can help us refine our vision—color it in and make it even better. A vision is strengthened by bringing in the viewpoints of many.

How are others involved in developing the vision? One good way to go about doing that is to start by making sure others on your team are on the same page. Do you share the same general values and goals? If so, it will be much easier to collaborate on a vision. Then each person will need to pray, listen to God, and contribute ideas and questions to the process of refining the vision. Each person should also think through questions about their own role in moving toward the vision: Am I a point person? Am I a helper? Am I behind-the-scenes or front-and-center? All of those roles are necessary, but each will need to be approached differently.

We are all needed, and we all need others.

To discover your own contribution, conduct a sober assessment of who you are: "For by the grace given me I say to every one of you: Do not think of yourself more highly than you ought, but rather think of yourself with sober judgment, in accordance with the faith God has distributed to each of you" (Romans 12:3). We are not to think of ourselves too highly—and falsely believe that we don't need others. And we are not to think of ourselves too lowly—and falsely believe that our contribution is not needed. We are all needed, and we all need others to minister together fully and well as the body of Christ. First we ask, "Who am I?" and then we ask, "Who do I need?"

PROVERBS:

✤ Proverbs 30:27: Locusts have no king, yet they advance together in ranks.

✤ Proverbs 20:18: Plans are established by seeking advice; so if you wage war, obtain guidance.

CHECKPOINTS:

Testing the vision

A vision that is inspired by God will require the power of God to fulfill it. Use the questions below to test the vision and help sharpen it.

❑ Is the vision appropriate for the group or organization?

❑ Does the vision motivate people to action?

❑ Will the vision require risk to fulfill?

❑ Does the vision promote faith?

❑ Does the vision glorify God?

For a vision to glorify God, it must be vitally connected to the heart of God. To what degree is the vision focused on what God is focused on?

PLANNING IN TEAMS

Once we have the basic vision, we can begin the planning. Here are some rules of thumb for planning any multi-step project:

- ✤ What has to happen? (list all items)
- ✤ What do we need to do first? (put the items in order)
- ✤ When does each item need to be completed? (assign dates)
- ✤ Who is best suited to do each item? (delegate each item to a specific person)
- ✤ What resources are available? (ensure that people have what they need to complete their tasks on time)
- ✤ How will we review progress and make midcourse corrections? (set follow-up appointments to celebrate progress and stay on track)

One helpful approach a team can use is called the post-it planning process (described below). Used well, it's a good—even fun—team exercise that yields a useful plan that is embraced by the whole team. In the years I (Bob) have worked with teams, this is one of the best exercises I've run across. It helps the visionary who doesn't do detail, as well as empowering people who see the little things but not the big picture. Overall, the post-it planning process can allow the body of Christ to come together to perform its various functions effectively.

POST-IT PLANNING PROCESS

1. Brainstorm important milestones during the first year. Write each one on a post-it note.
2. Arrange milestones in a logical sequence on a poster board(s) or white board. Add other milestones as you find gaps and/or missing tasks.
3. Identify the critical milestones.
4. Add a realistic timeline or rearrange milestones in a time-oriented sequence on the poster board or white board, maintaining the logical relationships.

5. Verify that each milestone has sufficient lead time for accomplishment.

6. Place asterisks by the tasks that could be delegated. Write in the names of the responsible people.

7. Determine additional resources necessary for the accomplishment of each milestone, for example, budget, materials, resources.

8. Complete reality checks.

   ✦ Is it consistent with values, mission, and ministry model?

   ✦ Are the projections realistic?

   ✦ Is there adequate personnel?

   ✦ Are there sufficient resources?

   ✦ Are all gaps identified?

Ten houses shared a common garden area. A couple that lived in one of the houses wanted to see flowers planted there. So Troy and Susan invited all of their neighbors over to have iced tea on their front porch to talk about what to do with the common area. Those who lived in three of the houses chose not to attend; they had no preference on the garden. But the residents of the rest of the houses gathered on the porch.

Troy and Susan began by sharing their vision for the garden: planting a variety of different types of flowers that would all bloom at different times of the summer so they would have flowers all summer long. Others added their own ideas: taller flowers toward the middle with shorter ones around the edges, balancing the colors of the flowers so there would be variety, planting some perennials that would bloom again every year.

Once the general vision was agreed upon, someone suggested that Susan and one other neighbor draw up a plan of what types of flowers would be planted where. They knew the most about gardening, so that made sense. Several other people who knew very little about gardening offered to dig holes and put the plants in where they were told. Two others offered to take up a collection and then go out to purchase the flower seeds and bulbs beforehand. One man offered his wheelbarrow and a few bags of potting soil. Then a date was set for the project.

Essentially, Troy and Susan facilitated a planning meeting to share their vision, hear all the ideas, and gain buy-in and commitment for the gardening project. From there, they created a plan with multiple steps. The result was a shared vision for the garden, a team of people working together to see that vision brought to reality, and everyone being able to enjoy the results of their work.

To live out our calling we need others alongside us. "From him [Christ] the whole body, joined and held together by every supporting ligament, grows and builds itself up in love, as each part does its work" (Ephesians 4:16). None of us is complete on our own; we were not designed to work alone. We all have different but essential parts to play, so we need to learn how to work well with others toward a shared vision.

■ ■ ■

Maria's conversation with the pastor didn't go in the direction she had expected. He listened with interest to all of her ideas and was patient as she described her interactions with Scott. But when she was finished, Pastor Tom said, "Excellent! I'm so glad you've got someone like Scott on your team. You'll really need him in order to move this ministry ahead."

Maria looked stunned. "Move ahead? But he's the one blocking it!" And Pastor Tom explained how the different parts of the body work together. He quoted from I Corinthians 12, explaining that a ministry of all eyes (like Maria and her vision) would lack the hands to actually ground the plan in reality and make sure the day-to-day work got done. She not only didn't need another pair of eyes—she needed Scott's hands. "But he just doesn't get it!" exclaimed Maria in exasperation.

"Well, I'm not saying you're working together effectively right now. All I said was that you need each other. And I think you also need someone else. Maybe a central nervous system to help with communication between the parts. You need someone who can see your vision and help you work on your communication with Scott. Somehow, I suspect you're not the only frustrated volunteer in this ministry area," he smiled. "Why don't you talk with Allison? She's Sarah's mom...one of the parents in the ministry. She might be able to sit down with you and Scott and facilitate a planning meeting. Obviously, the ministry is at a turning point, so it's a good time for a conversation anyway."

The following week, Maria, Scott, and Allison sat down together. Allison served almost as a translator by asking questions, "Maria, tell us more about what you want to see happen. What would be good about that? What would this approach accomplish? Scott, tell us more about your concerns? What areas of quality do you want to be sure we keep intact as the ministry grows? What are some ways we might do that?"

They walked away with a plan for the ministry that made use of both Maria's gifts and Scott's gifts—as well as leaving them with a greater understanding and appreciation of each other.

GROUP DISCUSSION QUESTIONS:

1. What are your spiritual gifts? What are you good at?
2. How do your gifts most contribute to the team's mission?
3. What is missing from your contribution that requires the input of other gifts?
4. What gifts do you tend to undervalue in others?
5. Name one specific way your gifts could be strengthened by working together with someone who is different than you.
6. Who do you sense God asking you to work alongside?
7. What would be the benefits of working with them?

SUGGESTED SCRIPTURE FOR MEMORIZATION:

For just as each of us has one body with many members, and these members do not all have the same function, so in Christ we, though many, form one body, and each member belongs to all the others. We have different gifts, according to the grace given to each of us. (Romans 12:4-6)

CHAPTER 13

The Kingdom Contribution

Sonya had come a long way. She had been faithful in learning to manage her money well, and she had learned more about how to spend time with God according to the way she was wired, not just according to some arbitrary standard. As her life became more sane and as she grew in her practices of solitude and serving, Sonya began wondering what else God might have in store for her. How could she make a lasting contribution to his kingdom?

Her volunteer work at the nursing home was rewarding, but it felt too small to her. Sonya knew it made a difference to the residents there, but she couldn't help but feel there was room to expand. She also enjoyed her accountability group and her job teaching high school social studies. She knew that she also made a difference in both of those places, especially with the kids who came from difficult backgrounds and needed some of the extra encouragement and help that she could give them.

Sonya was using her gifts. But was there a way she could use them on an even larger scale? And how could she know she was using them toward kingdom ends—toward something that would make a lasting difference in the kingdom of God? Sonya couldn't quite see an answer, but the questions kept nagging at her.

■ ■ ■

Once God has helped us put the pieces of our life together so we're not moving from crisis to crisis, it's like we reach a plateau. We look around and wonder what's next. Our gratitude to God for what he's done for us shifts our focus outward. And when we look outward, we see the vast needs that surround us: a world that needs to experience the love of Jesus in tangible ways, people that need to be freed from what imprisons them.

When we see the needs, we wonder how we can help. How can we make a real difference? What kind of tangible, lasting contribution to the kingdom can we make?

Someone once said that last words are lasting words. And what were the last recorded words Jesus spoke to his disciples?

> Then Jesus came to them and said, "All authority in heaven and on earth has been given to me. Therefore go and make disciples of all nations, baptizing them in the name of the Father and of the Son and of the Holy Spirit, and teaching them to obey everything I have commanded you. And surely I am with you always, to the very end of the age." (Matthew 28:18-20)

This is the mission he left them after his resurrection. Those words—known as the great commission—are words Jesus wanted us to remember. As disciples of Jesus, the ultimate contribution we can make is to play our part in the process of making more disciples.

That will look different for every person, according to their gifts, passions, and abilities, but we can all play a part in helping others experience authentic life with God and others.

The ultimate contribution we can make is to make more disciples.

What does it look like to make disciples?

The following five categories may be helpful in completing our understanding of what making disciples looks like:

- **Discern**: discovering in whom God is working
- **Explore**: having purposeful conversations about the gospel
- **Invite**: encouraging people to become followers of Jesus
- **Establish**: baptize and teach loving obedience to Jesus
- **Multiply**: help new followers make more followers

Let's unpack these five areas a bit more.

DISCERNING is keeping an eye and an ear open to take notice of where God is at work. He is always at work somewhere, and when we fully open our senses to discovering where that is, God will be revealed. We are not talking here about the spiritual gift of discernment, but the responsibility of all believers to stay attuned to what God is doing.

Discerning can look like:

- The man who befriends his coworkers and prays that God would allow him to see their spiritual needs.
- The woman who is part of a new moms' group and senses God at work in one of the other women there. As this second woman is navigating the changes of this new stage of life, she's begun asking questions about God and meaning and where to invest her energy—what will really matter? The first woman makes it a point to ask her to get coffee sometime so she can hear more of what's going on.

EXPLORING is engaging with others around their relationship with God. After we have discerned where and in whom God is at work, exploration of those possibilities is how we respond.

Exploring can look like:

- The woman who asks questions about the faiths of others and genuinely wants to learn what's behind those other belief systems.
- The pair of friends who allow their conversation to move beyond interpersonal relationships to their relationship with God.

✤ The couple who is getting together with another couple to read through the Gospel of John and talk about it.

INVITING means encouraging people to become followers of Jesus. Once we have discerned where God is at work, explored those relationships and listened well, we can then invite others to follow him.

Inviting can look like:

✤ The woman who, after months of spiritual conversations with her friend, asks, "So what's stopping you from trusting Jesus?" Her friend surprises herself with her own answer: "Nothing, I suppose. I do trust him. Jesus seems to be one of the most trustworthy people I've ever encountered."

✤ The man who leads Vacation Bible School and explains the way of Jesus to a group of six-year-olds.

✤ The man who prays with a coworker to receive Christ.

ESTABLISHING is what we do with new Christians to help them become rooted and grounded in Christ. We coach them toward development in both their personal lives and their ministry, and help them begin living out an expression of Christian community with others.

Establishing can look like:

✤ The woman who leads a discussion about baptism in her small group of new believers and encourages them to be baptized.

✤ The man who sets aside time every Friday morning to meet with a couple of friends who have just discovered Jesus. They read scripture together, pray together, and talk about what this journey is like so far.

MULTIPLYING means looking for those who are fruitful, investing in them, and connecting them with one another. The result is authentic communities of followers of Jesus being formed and multiplied, disciples resourced to be fruitful, leaders coached and connected to one another as they continue to multiply.

Multiplying can look like:

✤ The woman who, while discipling a new believer, includes a third person in that group—the new believer's friend, who has been asking "what this whole Jesus thing is about." The dialogue becomes multi-dimensional, growing and sharing at the same time, while maintaining open communication with both followers and non-followers of Jesus.

✤ The teenage boy who takes the risky step of telling his atheist parents about his new and growing relationship with Jesus.

✤ The waitress who, after coming to know Jesus, still maintains her friendships with other waiters and waitresses she has built relationships with.

CHECKPOINT:

To delve deeper into each of these five areas, ask each other these questions:

❏ In whom do you see God working?

❏ What conversations have you had about spiritual things?

❏ Who have you encouraged to become followers of Jesus?

❏ How are you helping new believers follow Jesus?

❏ How are you helping new followers make more followers?

When we are making disciples, we are helping to populate heaven.

As we make disciples, we try to discern in whom God is working, and we explore with them and invite them to discover more about Jesus. Simply put, we follow Jesus by living out the great commandment and the great commission. Our first goal is to serve as the hands and feet of Jesus to the world around us in obedience to the great commandment. Our second goal is to share the gospel and make disciples in obedience to the great commission.

CHECKPOINT:

❏ When we are making disciples, we are helping to populate heaven. Take some time alone and visualize the kingdom of heaven. All nations, all ethnic groups, all walks of life. As you look around, who's left out? Who should be there that you don't see? What are the missing groups of people who could be reached?

Cast your nets wide

Like Jesus, we are called to a broad approach as we reach out and engage with others—cast your nets widely, sow your seeds broadly, spread out your tents. We don't know who will be receptive and who won't be. That part is up to God, not us. We are called to love and to serve regardless of the response of others.

> Then he told them many things in parables, saying: "A farmer went out to sow his seed. As he was scattering the seed, some fell along the path, and the birds came and ate it up. Some fell on rocky places, where it did not have much soil. It sprang up quickly, because the soil was shallow. But when the sun came up, the plants were scorched, and they withered because they had no root. Other seed fell among thorns, which grew up and choked the plants. Still other seed fell on good soil, where it produced a crop—a hundred, sixty or thirty times what was sown. Whoever has ears, let them hear."

Our part is sharing the love of Jesus in tangible, relational was with all who are around us.

> "Listen then to what the parable of the sower means: When people hear the message about the kingdom and do not understand it, the evil one comes and snatches away what was sown in their hearts. This is the seed sown along the path. The seed falling on rocky ground refers to people who hear the word and at once receive it with joy. But since they have no root, they last only a short time. When trouble or persecution comes because of the word, they quickly fall away. The seed falling among the thorns refers to people who hear the word, but the worries of this life and the deceitfulness of wealth choke the word, making it unfruitful. But the seed falling on good soil refers to people who hear the word and understand it. They produce a crop, yielding a hundred, sixty or thirty times what was sown." (Matthew 13:3-9, 18-23)

Whether people are receptive to the message of Jesus is not up to us. That is up to God. Our part is sharing the love of Jesus in tangible, relational ways with all who are around us. We live like that regardless of the responses of others. But in living that way, some will respond and networks of people who follow Jesus will be created.

The goal has never been for one person to follow Jesus all alone. The goal is *communities* of people following Jesus together. As the message of Jesus is preached through our actions, it spreads throughout whole networks of people: "The kingdom of heaven is like yeast that a woman took and mixed into about sixty pounds of flour until it worked all through the dough" (Matthew 13:33).

As people come to know Jesus, his message spreads from one person to another through the natural networks of relationships that already exist. That's just how the early church grew. Together they became the hands and feet of Jesus to the world around them, as they continued to bring in others who wanted to experience Jesus. "Every day they continued to meet together in the temple courts. They broke bread in their homes and ate together with glad and sincere hearts, praising God and enjoying the favor of all the people. And the Lord added to their number daily those who were being saved" (Acts 2:46-47).

CHECKPOINT:

❏ How can you best create and strengthen networks of relationships? Write down three different strategies.

PROVERBS:

✤ Ecclesiastes 11:6: Sow your seed in the morning, and at evening let your hands not be idle, for you do not know which will succeed, whether this or that, or whether both will do equally well.

LOVE GOD, LOVE OTHERS, AND MAKE DISCIPLES ALONG THE WAY

Actions speak louder than words. That was true in Jesus' day and is still true in ours. Compassion is both the medium and the message. We don't need to hard-sell the gospel message. We can live it out and explain it in the context of relationships. As we live out the kingdom here on earth, people will begin to understand much better than they could by words alone.

We need to invite others into our lives in order to make that happen. In this way, the message of Jesus in words becomes a by-product of the way we live: we love God, we love others, and we make disciples as we go. People deciding to follow Jesus flows out of who we are and how we live, not just what we say.

Actions speak louder than words.

CHECKPOINT:

❏ Examine the great commandment (Matthew 22:37-40) and the great commission (Matthew 28:18-20). What relationships do you see between the two? List as many connections as you can.

PROVERBS:

✤ Proverbs 3:35: The wise inherit honor, but fools get only shame.

✤ Proverbs 4:6-9: Do not forsake wisdom, and she will protect you; love her, and she will watch over you. The beginning of wisdom is this: Get wisdom. Though it cost all you have, get understanding. Cherish her, and she will exalt you; embrace her, and she will honor you. She will give you a garland to grace your head and present you with a glorious crown.

✤ Proverbs 21:21: Whoever pursues righteousness and love finds life, prosperity and honor.

LEGACY

As we grow in our relationship with God, loving him and loving others, and helping more people become followers of Jesus, we leave a legacy. What kind of legacy do you want to leave? That's a question worth asking ourselves every year or so: "What legacy do I want to leave behind?" Legacy means a gift handed down from those who have gone before us. It can be property, money, a culture, values, a history. We will all leave this earth at some point and we will all leave a legacy. The question is what kind of legacy we want to leave for those who come after us. What we do now determines how we will be remembered.

As we invest all that God has given us, we try to do so wisely, making the most of what we have. For this is our legacy. This is what we will leave behind. This is our ultimate contribution to the kingdom of God. The apostle Paul explains it this way:

> Do you not know that in a race all the runners run, but only one gets the prize? Run in such a way as to get the prize. Everyone who competes in the games goes into strict training. They do it to get a crown that will not last; but we do it to get a crown that will last forever. Therefore I do not run like someone running aimlessly; I do not fight like a boxer beating the air. (1 Corinthians 9:24-26)

My (Bob's) father wrote this in a Bible that he gave me for my ninth grade graduation: "The most important part of a race is the finish—*never* let the goal out of your sight and you will steer a straight course all the way through life. Then you can happily repeat with Paul 'I have finished my course, I have kept the faith.' (2 Timothy 4:7)"

Love,
Mom and Dad

We are to run like we want to win. As we serve the world, we do so strategically, so as to love God, love others, and make disciples. We can each make our unique contribution to the kingdom of God by leaving our legacy. Ultimately, our legacy is our investment in the next generation: making a difference in the life of another, raising up and developing others who will continue to follow Jesus after we are gone.

Some of the most important fruit we leave behind will be a result of how we love.

Jesus implied that some of the most important fruit we leave behind will be a result of how we love:

You did not choose me, but I chose you and appointed you so that you might go and bear fruit—fruit that will last—and so that whatever you ask in my name the Father will give you. This is my command: Love each other. (John 15:16-17)

If we live well, as disciples of Christ, following his guidance, we will leave a legacy. We will make a difference in this world and in the lives of others. And someday, the Lord will say to us, "**Well done, good and faithful servant**! You have been faithful with a few things; I will put you in charge of many things. Come and share your master's happiness!" (Matthew 25:21).

■ ■ ■

Sonya had a legacy to leave.

One day when she was volunteering at the nursing home, an older gentleman named Bill told her, "I love hearing about the students you teach at your school. Ah, if I only knew then what I know now. I've found that much of what seemed to be so important back then really didn't matter much, while the things I took for granted then seem to be all I think about now. But now it feels like so long since I've even seen many young people, much less talked with them."

That got Sonya thinking. And it seemed so simple she wondered why she hadn't thought of it before. She was connected to two different groups of people that needed one another: teenagers and the elderly. She talked with students at school, not expecting much of a response. After all, many teenagers aren't aware that they need the elderly. But Sonya was pleasantly surprised.

Fifteen students accompanied her to the nursing home the following weekend—many of them kids she thought wouldn't be interested. But as she saw one boy sitting with Bill, the man whose comment last week had triggered her idea, she saw the power of different generations communicating with each other. She knew this boy's story, and she knew how much he needed older men in his life.

Over time, Sonya taught the students how to help out more and how to communicate more effectively with the residents in the nursing home. And she was surprised by how often spiritual topics of conversation came up. The residents had already lost many loved ones and were thinking about their own future, while the teenagers were curious and open to new ideas.

Not only had Sonya left a legacy, she had helped this man to leave one as well.

The time came when Sonya turned over this ministry to one of the members of her accountability group who she'd been training. This other woman was more gifted in administration and was passionate about the ministry Sonya had started. On Sonya's last day at that nursing home, she saw the same teenage boy sitting with Bill in front of a window watching it rain. They had developed a friendship, and the boy had come to know Jesus.

Not only had Sonya left a legacy, she had helped this man to leave one as well.

GROUP DISCUSSION QUESTIONS:

1. Given what you have, what are some ideas you have for making a contribution?
2. What are some of the most effective ways you could use of your time and energy?
3. What legacy do you hope to leave?

SUGGESTED SCRIPTURE FOR MEMORIZATION:

Do you not know that in a race all the runners run, but only one gets the prize? Run in such a way as to get the prize. Everyone who competes in the games goes into strict training. They do it to get a crown that will not last; but we do it to get a crown that will last forever. (1 Corinthians 9:24-25)

Appendix

Note to pastors: A plan for using *Making Life Count* in your church

Having people read this book in the context of small groups or discipling relationships is just one way to use it. If you want to implement *Making Life Count* on a churchwide scale, we've listed a step-by-step plan below for one way you can do that, supported by online resources. But feel free to get creative and come up with different ways to adapt the material to fit your church context.

ACTION PLAN STEPS:

1. Read through this book with your leadership team and work through the exercises and discussion questions to become acquainted with the material.

2. Introduce the idea to your congregation with a sermon that touches on the felt needs found in the introduction of this book.

3. Follow up after the sermon with a letter or email to people in the congregation inviting them to attend a gathering to discuss a plan for working through this book in community. For increased sociability and appeal, make it a potluck meal or a pizza night.

4. Order copies of *Making Life Count* in bulk to receive a discounted rate: www.churchsmart.com

5. Gather with those interested to discuss a course of action. Eat together, present a plan, and lay out clear follow-up steps.

6. Organize interested people into groups of three or four to meet weekly for thirteen weeks.

7. These gatherings of three or four people will meet weekly and go through one chapter of the book each week, using the discussion questions and exercises as a guide.

8. Deliver sermons that align with the topics being discussed in the groups each week.

9. Gather together all of the people reading through the book once a month for a meal. A few discussion questions about what they are learning through the process can help guide the conversation.

10. Plan for the next round of others who may want to go through the book together during the next ministry season.

SUPPORTING RESOURCES FOR THE STEPS LISTED ABOVE:

You can run this implementation process yourself or you can contact CoachNet and we can do it for you. If you'd like us to walk you through an implementation process customized for your church or denomination, complete with a live on-site Making Life Count seminar, contact us via www.coachnet.org.

The following supporting resources are available online at www.coachnet.org:

1. Sermon suggestions and help
2. Sample invitation letter
3. Introductory meeting agenda, talking points and handout
4. Discussion questions for dinner groups
5. Planning for round two

Once you've gone through *Making Life Count* in your church, you'll be ready to move full-force into leadership development. Check out *From Followers to Leaders*, also by Robert E. Logan and Tara Miller, for your next step on the path.

POSTSCRIPT:

We hope you've enjoyed walking alongside us as you've journeyed through this book. As we've been writing it's been fun to imagine you out there reading, thinking, and growing in your relationship with God and others. Our hope is you've become even more firmly committed to becoming a follower of Jesus—for it's only after we become followers that we can become leaders.

For those of you who are wondering what's next, check out *From Followers to Leaders: The Path of Leadership Development in the Local Church.*

From Followers to Leaders:
The Path of Leadership Development in the Local Church

by Robert E. Logan
and Tara Miller

ISBN#: 1-889638-69-2

Published by ChurchSmart Resources